TOTIS

TOTIS

J JOSEPH KAZDEN

ISBN: 1515203549
ISBN 13: 9781515203544
Library of Congress Control Number: 2015911888
CreateSpace Independent Publishing Platform
North Charleston, South Carolina

For Mary and Nora,
who inspire me daily

Already a Problem!

Reality is merely an illusion, albeit a very persistent one.
—Albert Einstein

The only reason for time is so that everything doesn't happen at once.
—Albert Einstein

TABLE OF CONTENTS

exception. Biology's experience of time's flow is future flowing past a present moment into a past. Only the present seems to exist, but the organism is not in sync with the present. Everything being experienced has already happened. It is difficult to break our total belief that our experience describes reality perfectly.

Meaning is a biological experience; the physical properties of the universe, such as mass and wavelength, have no meaning.

This is a discussion of quantum mechanics, including state changes, the uncertainty principle, wave particle duality, hidden variables, the double-slit experiment with its modern variants, the Einstein Podolsky Rosen (EPR) thought experiment, Bell's theorem, entanglement, and no hidden variables to explain "spooky action at a distance."

Human experience is an interpretation of reality and not actual reality itself. It is prone to inaccuracies and inconsistencies that are revealed as cognitive illusions. Three classes of illusions are defined: imperfect, perfect, and creative. A prime system of sensory interpretation is defined. The prime system and the systems that produce the illusory experiences are all part of the same class and operate in the same manner.

We do not measure time, we measure state changes using measuring tools with arbitrary meters. There is no universal constant "tick" of a clock. There is no universal "now" moment. Anthropocentrism and our inability to experience the true nature of time are discussed. All experiments have one common denominator, an observer. Our experience of the universe does not exist when we're not looking, but the true universe does. The action of entangled particle pairs in null time is explored. Michaelson Morley experiment and the 'luminiferous aether.' The universe is a quantum entity. The entire universe and everything in it, including all time, appeared in null time. Like Schrödinger's famous cat, it both is and is not, simultaneously (its beginning and end exist simultaneously). Time does not tick; it acts to solidify the universe in a stable unity, a totIs.

Our experience does not change the nature of reality; time does not flow—it is. The energy content of the totIs universe is zero. When we speak of "we," it is the observer that is meant. We require a now to exist, which is a biological interpretation of reality. We cannot transcend the very process by which we, the observer, exist.

Free will and its meaning are a purely human concern and are a consequence of our experience of time's arrow. We have a deep need to reinforce our experience of reality and to quarantine it from anything that may shatter it. We cannot abandon our experience of reality, but we can accept it as an illusion of sorts.

Mathematics, like time, is a biological construct. In a totIs universe, where time does not flow and all exists at once, mathematics descriptions are meaningless. AntIs is defined as the human observer's experience of reality through the biochemical sensory input and interpretation system. It also describes the near-perfect illusion this creates and our continuous attempts to use this interpretation as a proxy for actual reality.

For the observer, his or her viewpoint—and, thus, consciousness—is the center of reality. The nature of totIs space-time is discussed. Photons traveling in a vacuum collapse space-time to null values. An exercise of trying to consciously imagine a totIs universe is attempted.

PREFACE

Albert Einstein once famously said, "Reality is merely an illusion, albeit a very persistent one." This book is an exploration and illumination of the nature of that illusion and the true nature of reality itself. In order to make the arguments in this book readable and accessible to a wider audience, I've reprised the form Plato used to make his arguments in his book *The Republic*. And like *The Republic*, this book is written so that the chapters should be read in the order presented, as the ideas build and develop chapter by chapter. In my book, *totIs*, Socrates walks among us again, but, in this symposium, the discoveries of modern science are available to the characters involved. I have given Greek names to the characters, but they are from transliterated Greek words that are related, though sometimes obscurely, to important scientists who laid the groundwork for our modern world. The characters are as follows: Socrates, as himself; Geraki, meaning 'hawk', for Steven Hawking; Miapetra, meaning 'one stone', for Albert Einstein; Ankistro, meaning 'hook', for Robert Hooke; Nikitis, meaning 'winner', for Leonardo DaVinci; Oachyronas, meaning 'barn', for Joseph-Louis Lagrange; Neatono, meaning 'new ton', for Isaac Newton; and Sanida, meaning 'plank', for Max Plank. None of the characters in this book actually represent any of the abovementioned scientists or any other person, living or dead; rather, this book's entire company combines and synthesizes their thoughts and the thoughts of many others who have contributed to our understanding of ourselves, our world, and the universe we live in. Standing on the shoulders of these creative giants and gazing out over the landscape they have surveyed, I recognize the great debt and gratitude owed to them.

ONE

I went down to the harbor yesterday with Miapetra, son of Sanida, to congratulate the harbor master for his inauguration of the new Festival of Poseidon. I was also curious to see the many beautifully decorated and strangely regaled boats taking part in this sea parade. The variety and ingenuity on display enthralled me, and I found it thoroughly entertaining, especially on such a perfect day as this. The sky was nearly cloudless, the temperature was benign, and the bright sunlight glinted like diamonds off the wind-cut facets that rippled on the restless water.

My friend Miapetra turned to me and said, "Socrates, I have often mused that the patterning of the sunlight dancing across the water, as it is now, might be encoded with hidden information, containing the key to revealing the greatest secrets of the universe. Unfortunately, that possibility seems always obscured by the unfathomable probabilities brought together by wind, water, light, and a host of other forces to produce these transfixing scenes. Yet here they are, in fact, actually being produced."

"Miapetra," I said, "if I were to ask you to predict the exact patterning of light on the water exactly one second from now, and then again one second later, and again, and again, second by second, what would you say?"

"I would say it would be nigh impossible," said Miapetra, "given the complexity of the problem, as I just mentioned. The best that can be done would be to predict the probability of some patterns occurring."

"And yet," I said, "in one second that actual pattern will appear, and the second after that, and so on and so on."

"You must agree though," said Miapetra, "that the laws of probability are used with great effect to predict outcomes of events, to predict the future with great precision."

"That is true," I replied. "But, at the same time, these laws befuddle us, because we are never able to predict the exact fate of any single particular or particle being followed in these analyses. The probabilistic laws seem to encapsulate all, from the tiniest quantum-mechanical particle to the largest structures in the universe, and though their predictive power is profound, the inability to predict the outcomes for specific objects and/or events remains a troubling obscurity."

"That is clearly true," said Miapetra.

"You agree then that probabilities and their laws are valid and useful for predicting outcomes in the future."

"I would."

"And would you also agree that the same would hold true for the past?"

"How do you mean, Socrates?" Miapetra replied. "If the past has already occurred, we know the actual outcome itself."

"True enough," I said, "but though we may have the information contained in an actual outcome—say a photograph of this glimmering sea—we are unaware of the actual forces that produced the pattern and could use probability's laws to predict with some precision what forces were at play in producing the pictured pattern."

"That is true," said Miapetra. "Probability is a useful predictive tool for both the past and the future."

"So we can say that probability's efficacy lies in its ability to predict with some accuracy events and forces that emanate from the future or the past."

"We can indeed say that."

"But we do not live in the past or future. We live in a 'now' moment, where events and outcomes become actual."

"That is obvious," said Miapetra.

"So would you agree then that probability meets its end when the items upon which our analysis is working have run their course and have done what we were predicting they would eventually do—a state we can call manifest reality?"

"I would, Socrates."

"For simplicity's sake, in continuing to talk about probability and manifest reality, I will use the word *future* to mean any time not part of a manifest reality—that is, the now—if you will allow me to," I said.

"From now on, when you use the word *future,* I will understand that you are referring to any time not part of manifest reality," replied Miapetra.

"So it follows," I continued, "that probability and manifest reality are different but related things, does it not?"

"It does."

"And would you agree that probability is dependent on manifest reality, whereas manifest reality is not dependent on probability?"

"That sounds correct," said Miapetra, "but can you explain it further?"

"I will try my best," I said. "If one thing is dependent on the existence of another thing, then one would be the prime thing and the other the dependent. In such a case, the prime thing does not rely on the dependent thing for its existence, but the dependent relies on the prime for its existence. For instance, take your hair. It is the prime thing, and its color the dependent thing. Descriptions of the color of your hair are meaningless inasmuch as they depend on the reality of your hair in the first place. That you have hair is the prime fact, and its color is dependent on that fact."

"Yes, I see that clearly now."

"So, in the case of probability and manifest reality, it would follow that probability is the dependent thing and manifest reality is the prime thing. Manifest reality does not rely on probability for its existence, whereas probability's usefulness, if you will, depends entirely on manifest reality. It would be meaningless to ask what the probability is that I am a dog, except as some sort of mathematical mind game whose outcome has no value except as a diversion or party entertainment. Probability is an abstract construct whose very existence depends on the nature of manifest reality."

"Your reasoning leaves no doubt," said Miapetra.

"So then, probability only exists with respect to an unknown future. It would appear that this future does not yet exist but will ineluctably flow into the now that is before our eyes. In the universe we experience, things happened in the past, things are happening all around us now, in the present, and things will happen in the future. What ties this scenario together is time itself and the fact that time seems to have a direction, a movement from the past to the future. This is what gives probability any predictive power at all. It is not, however, the removal of time that collapses probability but manifest reality emerging with the passage of time. Perhaps, Miapetra, this is a piece of the hidden information you sense when the sunlight's pattern is dancing across the rippling waters."

"Perhaps it is," replied Miapetra. "Your discourse has begun to give some solidity to my evanescent musings."

TWO

As Miapetra was speaking, I caught sight of Ankistro, son of Neatono, waving from a distance as he came toward us. Upon reaching us, Ankistro said to me, "I see you and your companion have been enjoying the regatta this fine day."

"Indeed we have," I replied.

"Well, there is another celebration today, that of my father, and your old friend, Neatono, whom you seem to be avoiding as of late."

"Avoiding, no, but remiss in not visiting more, I am sorry to say, yes. I have been forced to attend to many pressing problems above all other concerns these past two years and have missed my visits with your father as well as with my other friends."

As I spoke, Ankistro waved over two of his friends, the brothers Nikitis and Oachyronas.

"Socrates," cried Nikitis, as he and his brother joined our little party. "Surely you and Miapetra will join us to help Neatono celebrate his birthday."

"Indeed, as he ages, my father frets about time and its swift passing," said Ankistro.

"Socrates has been enlightening me on some of the properties of time and its relationship with probability," said Miapetra. "Perhaps he might be able to enlighten Neatono as well and help allay some of his worries."

"I might just as well add to his worries," I said, "but it has been too long since I've seen my old friend, and to help celebrate his birthday would be a great pleasure."

"Then it is settled," said Ankistro. "You can join us now, as we make our way to my father's house atop the hill. My father's preoccupation with time has led him to study some of its properties, and I'm sure he will be most interested in speaking on the subject with such a learned man as you, Socrates."

"And I with him," I said, as we started off to Neatono's house on the hill.

THREE

Accordingly, we followed Ankistro to his father's house and there found Neatono and his youngest son, Geraki. Miapetra's father, Sanida, was there as well, as he and Neatono studied together at the university and had kept a long and close friendship going ever since. Sanida was soundly sleeping on a sofa near the wall. Filtered sunlight filled the room, and a warm and convivial atmosphere prevailed.

"How now," cried Neatono, "it is my old friend Socrates, whom I have despaired in ever seeing again!"

"My dear friend," I replied. "I apologize for my long absence from your home and beg forgiveness for it. As you may have heard, I have been preoccupied with some legal troubles in the east, which have eaten up my time and energy as of late, leaving little left for the enjoyment of life and time with one's dearest friends."

"Socrates, I have indeed heard," said Neatono. "It has been a stone in my soul that I could not be of any help to you, but age has been less kind than youth, and I have found the need to remain close to my home and family these days."

"I think that Father has been trying to fool time by hiding out here at home," said Geraki, "in the hopes that its inevitable ravages will lose sight of him and leave him in peace."

"My son is still hale, and the passions of the body still call strongly to him, but, for an old man like me, the pleasures I lean toward lie in contemplation and conversation. I pray, Socrates, that you will make yourself at home here as often as you wish, as we are old friends, and I relish and miss your company."

"I should like nothing better and have always felt at home and at ease here, my dear Neatono," I said. "Our conversations have always been both a source of pleasure and most enlightening to me."

Geraki spoke up now and said, "Father has been investigating the properties of time and has spent many hours reading on the subject. Unfortunately, my brother and I spend our time studying music and gymnastics in order to better ourselves and to be useful to our family and our state. I'm glad you are here to engage him in some conversation on this subject."

"I am old and getting older," replied Neatono, "and though I know I cannot stop the swift arrow of time, I find it interesting how my experience of time has shifted as I've aged."

"How so?" I asked.

"It seemed to me that as a young man a day would last forever, a week became an interminable length of time, and a month seemed an eternity. Now the days flash by like strokes of lightning, weeks and months run by as if in a race, and years slip by like sand between my fingers. How can my experience of time, which to the clock is so perfectly metered, feel so different to me according to my age?"

"This is a most interesting question," I replied. "It has been noted that persons nearby, or involved in, violent accidents report that time seems to slow to a trickle, and that they watch the horrid spectacle as if in slow motion. Alternatively, it is said that those who are drowning will experience the whole of their lives flash before their eyes in an instant, as if the time that comprised all those decades was being compressed into mere seconds. Pray tell me, Neatono, what it is you've discovered thus far."

"I began with a study of clocks and clock making, but quickly realized this has nothing at all to do with the nature of time but with creating machines with which to simply measure it, as a ruler measures space. It is a study of craft and materials and was of no interest to me."

"Indeed," I said. "Many confuse the measure of time for time itself, all the while having no conception of time's true nature."

"Very true," he said. "I then began a study of Einstein's theory of relativity. Unlike the ideas of old where time was considered to be a universal constant that stood alone and imperious, Einstein showed that time, far from independent, was inextricably linked to space itself, which is now called space-time, a continuous structure permeating the universe that both affects and is affected by matter and energy. Now objects moving through and events happening in space-time must be described in these four dimensions together. Stranger still, two observers with identical clocks moving through this space-time at different speeds and directions will not agree as to the time it takes for each clock to tick off each second."

The younger men, who, moments ago, were talking and joking among themselves, were suddenly silent with puzzled looks on their faces as they listened to Neatono's description.

"This is very unsettling," said Oachyronas, as his brother nodded in assent. "Surely the runners at the Olympic races are using the same clock with which to measure the results. If each had his own clock, would they not agree?"

"Einstein showed that at the speeds we mere mortals move, the effects are so small as to be unmeasurable," replied Neatono.

"However, with objects moving at large fractions of the speed of light or if they are near massive gravitational fields such as a black hole, these effects are very great indeed," I said.

"But how does that work?" asked Nikitis.

"How do we know if two things happen at the same time?" I asked Nikitis.

"Well, we can observe them happening using a stopwatch, just as at a race. If we observe both happening when we stop our timer, then they've happened at the same time," Nikitis responded.

"So then you would agree that simultaneity is defined by time and specifically is two or more things happening at the exact same time?" I asked.

"Yes, that is true," said Nikitis.

"Well," I continued, "Einstein has shown, through the theory of relativity, that observers moving through space at different speeds will not agree on whether events occur simultaneously."

"Not only that," added Neatono, "but the same is true in gravitational fields. Relative to two observers, time slows down if one is near a larger gravitational field than another."

Oachyronas said, "But isn't this just about the clocks?"

"No," said Neatono. "If I were to fly away from here at eight-tenths the speed of light to a star four light years away and then immediately return, ten years will have passed here on Earth. However, when I descend from my ship, I will have been traveling for only six years, according to my clock and body."

"Well then, let's get you aboard this spaceship and let you live longer," said Ankistro.

"No," said Neatono. "I will have aged more slowly relative to you here on Earth, but to me it will feel exactly the same as if I were aging right here with you. My reference frame does not constitute a fountain of youth. It simply shows that there is no magic spot in the universe from which all other time or space measurements can be made; all are relative to one another."

"Since we can no longer separate space and time, all objects and events must be described in these four dimensions," I said. "Now, so-called stationary objects are still in motion through time, and that motion is located in a reference frame of space-time. All objects and events that share that reference frame can agree on simultaneity, and only those objects and events. Objects and events moving in different directions and speeds occupy a different reference frame and so will not be able to agree on simultaneity."

At this point, Miapetra asked, "So are you saying that when we occupy different reference frames relative to one another that we can't agree on what is now?"

"That is correct," I said. "Indeed, my reference frame may intersect space-time at a point in your future or past relative to my own. But that is not all," I added. "Objects moving through space-time contract in length along the axis of their movement relative to other reference planes."

"This is all very strange and does not comport at all with the way I experience this world we live in," said Miapetra.

"Well it gets even stranger," I said. "It is difficult to picture an object that represents the three dimensions of space moving through time, but if we represent the three dimensions of space using a two-dimensional plane with the fourth dimension of time represented by the length of many planes in procession along this direction, we end with a solid block."

"I like the image of a loaf of bread," said Neatono, "as imagined by Brian Greene in his excellent book *The Fabric of the Cosmos*."

"Yes," I said, "it is an excellent metaphor, because the loaf of bread is a plastic sort of material and, like space-time, will warp with the inclusion of gravitational bodies and energy itself.

"Do you all understand that the light from distant stars can take millions and billions of years to reach us here on Earth?" I asked. "Meaning that the stars we're looking at are not actually in the position we see them and may indeed not even exist anymore."

"Yes, we do," came the chorus.

"Good," I continued, "and can you also accept that the reference frames that objects occupy by reason of their movement through space-time extend throughout the entire breadth of space-time?"

"We can," they said.

"Then I will describe the metaphor Mr. Greene used in his book to describe the incongruity of what we call a now moment. Try to imagine two planets in space-time separated by ten billion light years that are, to all intents and purposes, traveling on the same reference frame. That means that even though it will take the light from the far-off planet ten billion years to reach us, it is still stationary with respect to our Earth as we are both moving through space-time together at the same speed and in the same direction. Though far apart, we can, in theory, agree on the simultaneity of events on this broad reference frame, just as if it were right next to us."

They nodded in agreement.

"Socrates," said Neatono, "I have read this book and know that, for all of us to understand the metaphor, we need to understand that reference frames in space-time are measured relative to one another in that the angles they comprise in space-time are rotated. Therefore, if you were to 'slice' one observer's reference frame in space-time and also 'slice' another observer's, whose speed and direction are different, the two 'slices' of space-time would be at different angles to each other and would thus intersect at different past or future points in the time axis. They would not occupy the same 'now' time and so could not agree on simultaneity."

"Thank you, Neatono," I said. "If everyone understands this idea, then I will continue."

All nodded, though I thought I spied some consternation on a few faces.

"To report to you Brian Greene's metaphor of the space-time loaf of bread, I will need to refer to the reference frames of actual space-time as 'slices' in the 'loaf' representation he uses. Each slice through the loaf represents a reference frame on which objects are stationary relative to one another through space-time and thus agree on simultaneity. In other words, they occupy the same 'now' slice of space-time.

"The effects that will be described occur because, even though the relative movements of the observers occur at the same velocities we're used to in everyday life, the vast distances accentuate the imperceptible rotation of reference frames and thus give us very unusual results.

"Now, let us imagine two observers on our two planets who are also stationary relative to one another and thus occupying the same slice of space-time, even though they're so far apart. Their now moments are synchronous. If one gets up and moves away from the other at ten miles per hour, the slice of space-time she occupies and the 'now' it describes as her 'now' rotates to become synchronous with events that are one hundred fifty years in the past of the unmoving person. Likewise, a movement toward the unmoving observer will shift the mover's slice of space-time so that her 'now' slice crosses the loaf one hundred fifty years in the stationary observer's future, a future that the stationary person has no way of knowing about. Multiply the speed by one hundred, to one thousand miles per hour, and the 'now' slice of space-time is fifteen thousand years in the past or the future of the stationary observer as occupied by the moving person."

As I related this information, Miapetra grew suddenly excited.

"Socrates," he said, "do you realize what this means?"

"The ramifications of these effects range far and wide," I replied.

"Yes," he said, "but as it relates to what we were discussing earlier today at the regatta, according to these effects, in the moving observer's frame there are no probabilities with respect to the unmoving observer. Events have already unfolded and their outcomes are a matter of fact. Yet to the unmoving observer, the events that will occur in one hundred fifty years are unknowable."

"Yes, son, you are astute," said Sanida, who was now awake and joining in the conversation. "However, you must realize that the moving observer can receive no information she can use or share in her frame of reference vis-à-vis the unmoving observer, as it will take ten billion years for any information to reach her."

"True, my good friend Sanida," I said. "But his point that her frame of reference is nonetheless intersecting a space-time slice that is in the unknown future of this distant observer is an important one."

FOUR

"Socrates," Sanida said, "these effects go against our perceived reality, this conception of time is simply too foreign for us to accept, even when the physics says it is so."

Neatono joined in. "I have read that the physicist Paul Davies has said, 'Indeed, physicists insist that time doesn't flow at all; it merely is.'"

"If the physics is correct," said Sanida, "then why does time seem to have this arrow of motion? Why do we grow older and not younger?"

"What truth could be more unassailable than that time has an arrow where the future becomes the present and recedes into the past?" said Neatono.

"Perhaps," I said. "What is at odds with the physics is our experience of time."

"How do you mean?" asked Neatono.

"If I were to ask you whether something was sweet or salty, how could you discover that?" I asked.

"I would taste it," he said.

"And, likewise, if I asked you whether a certain tub of water were warm or cold, how could you find out?"

"I would feel it."

"And if I asked if it were day or night?"

"I would look outside, of course, and see for myself," he replied.

"And what is the mechanism by which you accomplish these acts?" I asked.

"They are the products of our sensory system," Neatono replied.

"So could you say that any and all physical states we can discern are subsets of a larger set called 'sense'?" I asked.

"That is accurate. You could say that," he replied.

"So I could just as accurately say I sensed the sweetness, or I sensed the heat, or I sensed the light?"

"You could indeed," he said.

"Could you also claim to have 'experienced' sweetness or 'experienced' the heat or 'experienced' the light without changing the meaning?" I asked.

At this point Sanida jumped in. "You could only if you were referring to the use of the sensory apparatus in particular to gain a knowledge or understanding of it. I believe that if you describe something, using the word *experience*, it usually means using more than one sense over a prolonged period of time."

"But, would you agree that, at its base, I could say that I tasted something sweet, or I sensed something sweet, or I experienced something sweet, and they would all be understood in the same way, notwithstanding any poetic usage?" I asked.

"I would say that you could most certainly do that," replied Sanida.

"What is your concern in asking this?" said Neatono.

"My concern is that these words can have other meanings and can be used in many different ways, but, for my purposes in exploring the nature of time, I will use these words in the strict sense I've defined here," I said.

"I see," said Sanida. "So that we may follow your reasoning, we must understand the exact meaning of your words."

"Yes," I said. "When I use the word *experience*, I mean an organism's interpretation of reality, which is the created product of our central nervous system, using the input of our sensory systems, such as touch, taste, smell, et cetera."

"So this is a scientific definition of an organism's turning sensory input into an experience of reality, as it exists around it," said Sanida.

"That is correct," I said. "And is there a product that comes from these senses, these experiences?" I asked.

"The product would be an awareness or understanding of our environment and ourselves in it," said Sanida.

"And how would you say we go about understanding the products of our sensory inputs?" I asked.

Neatono replied, "In the most elemental way, Socrates, we would first have to be conscious of them, to observe them—then we could remember them and ultimately learn from them."

"So would you agree that it is accurate to state that the products of our sensory apparatus are used by an 'observer' to ascertain and learn about his or her own state and the state of the environment?" I asked.

"That would be most accurate," he replied.

"And would you agree that the words *observer* and *perceiver* can be understood as the same thing when used in this way?" I asked.

"Indeed they can," he replied.

"And would you further agree that, to be an observer or perceiver, we are necessarily talking about a conscious being as opposed to an inanimate object?" I asked.

"That would be obvious," replied Sanida, "for there is no evidence that either rocks or stars exhibit any consciousness; only living beings have this gift."

"And does this *gift*, as you call it, rise to the level of a property of nature?" I asked. "Properties such as mass, wavelength, force, or energy."

"There is no proof that it does." Replied Sanida

"The nature of consciousness, and, thus, observers is a mystery," said Neatono, "But we know that living beings are, by their nature, organic and biological beings as opposed to the vast majority of elemental and inorganic material that makes up the universe," said Neatono.

"Good," I said. "Now we can move on to an exploration of the nature of experience.

"Sandia, you have studied biology and anatomy, what do we know about biological entities on this planet?" I asked.

"We know that the variety of biological entities is vast and varied, from single-celled organisms to incredibly complex multicellular creatures that contain whole colonies of other independent organisms that live and thrive in their own niche worlds, both symbiotically and parasitically. We also know that these organisms all have some sort of sensory system so as to engage with their environment, from the most rudimentary sensory system to the incredibly complex neurological system in species like our own," he said.

"And would you say these organisms experience their environments in the same way?" I asked.

"Definitely not," he replied. "The organisms on this planet cover a vast array of environmental diversity, from hyperthermophile bacteria that live in waters at temperatures of two hundred degrees Fahrenheit to emperor penguins that survive in the Antarctic winter with temperatures to minus forty degrees Fahrenheit, to give just a couple of examples."

"And would you agree that the hyperthermophile bacteria's experience in the two-hundred-degree water would be quite different than the penguins'?" I asked.

"Undoubtedly so," he replied. "The bacteria would experience well-being, while the penguins would experience great pain and death if they did not remove themselves from such an environment, and vice versa."

"So it would be accurate to say that, while biological diversity covers just about every variety and niche on the planet, each entity is, by design, capable of thriving in a narrow range of physical conditions?" I asked.

"I would say that is quite accurate," Sanida replied.

"And would you say that the sensory input systems in these entities are as varied as the biology that possesses them?" I asked.

"Definitely," he said. "There are creatures that taste with their feet, creatures that produce and hear radio waves, ones that see in the ultraviolet range, and some that see only black and white, while many don't see at all—with eyes, that is—and some that produce electrical charges, and some that echolocate. The variety is astoundingly large."

"We could discuss this topic for a very long time and not tire of finding new and exciting knowledge, but, for brevity's sake, I'd like to turn to the specific subject of human biology, because I have followed this line of questioning in search of the human experience of time," I said.

"So be it!" cried Nikitis and Oachyronas.

"This is all very interesting," Nikitis added, "but we are most interested in what you have to say about these strange properties of time and space."

"And that is where we're headed," I said. "But we must still explore the nature of experience in our own species, as we have narrowly defined it, for it is we who are asking these questions and not the amoeba or penguins."

"Will this take long?" asked Nikitis.

"As long as we need, for if we skip steps," I said, "we may stumble and fall and thus fail to discover whether the nature of the human experience of time may be at odds with the nature of time as expressed in physics. I suggest, my dear boys, that, if you have need of some diversion in the meantime, you can open a bottle of wine. Indeed, I would not mind a glass myself."

"I will do as you instruct, if Neatono will allow it," Nikitis said.

"Please do and, Ankistro, bring glasses all around," said Neatono. "You know where the good wine is. Bring that and pass by the ordinary stuff."

While the brothers went to the cellar to fetch the wine, Ankistro went to the cupboard to bring the goblets. In the meantime, the rest of us arose to stretch and move our limbs, stiff from sitting. In a few moments, the bottles were opened and the wine poured. We toasted to one another's health, happiness, and prosperity and thanked Neatono for his fine hospitality.

"This is indeed a fine vintage," said Sanida.

"And how can you tell that?" I asked.

"Ha," Sanida said with a laugh. "I can taste it, which of course means I am experiencing it."

"Well perhaps, my learned friend, you can enlighten our group on the very process that allows it," I said.

"Very well," he replied, "but let me warn you that a man or woman could spend an entire career on just one minuscule aspect of the process—for instance the process of neuronal communication or the specialization of retinal nerve cells."

"What we need," I said, "is an overview of the process that creates an experience out of sensory data. I think we can agree that it is based on a biochemical process, the minutia of which we can save for another discussion."

Sanida replied, "Very well, and you are correct, it is a complex biochemical process, which also includes a bioelectrical process, whereby sensory inputs are sent to the brain, or, to be more specific, the central nervous system, and there processed, which creates an experience. This process goes on continually, whether we are aware of it or not. Even a comatose or sleeping individual's central nervous system is processing stimuli."

"And would you agree that the reason this process occurs is for the survival of the organism?" I asked.

"Most assuredly," he replied, "for though we can experience many pleasurable and satisfying feelings, without this system in place and functioning, the organism perishes."

"And so this system not only receives information for processing, it also sends information in the form of commands to the body to initiate action," I said. "Is this correct?"

"Yes, indeed," replied Sanida. "Fight or flight, eating when hungry, drinking when thirsty—I think we are all aware of the multiplicity of urges, feelings, and desires upon which we act. It is called the central nervous system, because it is central to every one of them."

"And would you agree that the quality of the experience is dependent on the quality of the sensory stimuli supplied?" I asked.

"Well certainly there is a great diversity in the quality of sensory equipment across the individuals in any population. Some can hear a pin drop, when others hear nothing. Some see faraway objects, others can see tiny things, and yet others need glasses to see anything at all. It goes on and on. The quality of sensory input is quite varied, and the stimuli it supplies will affect the quality of the experience the organism can create," he said.

"So two individuals of the same species with sensory equipment of unequal quality will experience differently the same reality, to all intents and purposes, would you agree?" I asked.

"Yes, that is true," he responded.

"And what about the range of stimuli available to the organism—is it unlimited or limited?" I asked.

"It is very limited," he replied. "Sight, hearing, smell—all the sensory mechanisms respond to only a limited set of possible inputs. This is because the environment we can survive in is also very limited, and its requirements are very specific. For instance, the range of temperatures within which we can survive is a pinprick compared with the range of temperatures that exist in the universe. All the senses serve the organism in the limited environment in which they survive," he said.

"And where exactly does the sensory equipment get its data from?" I asked.

"From our environment in the world around us, obviously," he replied.

"And is it a real world or an imaginary world?" I asked.

"Though it may be an environment of limited range, representing a tiny fraction of the many different environments extant in the universe, it is still real," he replied.

"So then I think we can agree that our experience of the world around us is based on reality, albeit a limited slice of the total reality," I said.

All nodded in agreement.

"And would you also agree that the stimuli themselves are not the same thing as that which they are sensing?" I asked. "That the stimulus reports on reality but is not the reality itself?"

Geraki spoke up. "I can agree that the sensory apparatus react to specific and real attributes of the universe such as heat or light, but what the sensory apparatus sends is an encoded signal about that attribute, which is not the same thing as the attribute itself. But what of a rock that has fallen from a high place and landed on my foot, smashing it, breaking bones, and tearing flesh?" asked Geraki. "Is this not a real effect of an actual force directly affecting our bodies?"

"Our bodies, too, are real and are subject to the effects of the real world, but tell me, Geraki, what is the effect of a rock falling on the earth, or in the sea?" I asked.

"No harm is done as far as the earth or sea are concerned," he replied.

"And what if a falling rock should break another rock in half or cause a hole to form in the earth?" I asked.

"These are inanimate objects that have no senses to feel, nor any reason to do so," he said.

"But, to a living organism, this and other forces can compromise its integrity, which could lead to the destruction of its life," I said. "The force itself is meaningless; it has no wish to harm a biological entity, but the organism's experience of that force is interpreted as life altering and/or threatening. The sensations of pain we experience are not created by the rock. They are created by our central nervous system as an interpretation of the effects of the rock on our flesh, so that we may be aware of it," I said.

"And would you agree that the means of stimulus processing in the central nervous system to create an experience for the organism is, in effect, a manufactured interpretation of reality?" I asked.

"I would have to say it is so," said Geraki.

"And would you agree that an interpretation of a thing is not the same thing as the thing itself, especially when the information used for the interpretation is both limited and is itself already processed?" I asked.

"Again, I cannot argue with that statement," said Geraki.

"Then given what we've discovered thus far, can we conclude that our experience of reality is a biochemical interpretation? That this experience is composed of only a portion of reality that is supplied to our central nervous system by sensory apparatuses of limited sensitivity? That the signals from these apparatuses to the central nervous system are biochemical artifacts themselves, and that the main function of this process is the survival of the organism?" I asked.

"I think we can agree that your description is accurate," said Geraki.

"Furthermore, can we say that, though we may believe our central nervous system's interpretation to be reality itself, it is not?" I asked.

"We must agree again," said Geraki.

"As observers then, we do not so much live in the world as create an experience of a world we live in, and, on the whole, it functions beautifully within the limited scope of the physical conditions within which our biology can survive. This describes a biochemically driven closed-loop system whose function is to ensure the survival of the organism. As an experience of the organism, it is what we call life," I concluded.

FIVE

"So now, my friends, though we have not proven that time, as described by physics, describes its reality, we have at least called into question our own experience and interpretation of the nature of time," I said.

"But what choice do we have?" asked Neatono. "For us, the experience of life is reality, to all intents and purposes."

"That is true if we wish to blindly accept such, but it is my purpose to shed some light in an area of darkness and obscurity, if you are willing to follow along," I said.

"I think it promises to be a difficult and perhaps perilous journey," he said.

"Perhaps," I said, "but, nonetheless, a journey well worth taking, for what is more exciting for people of learning than to discover, using their minds, that which is hidden before them?"

"I'm willing to take this journey," said Miapetra.

"As am I," said Geraki.

"Indeed, I think we all are," said Sanida. "So lead on, dear Socrates."

"Then let us start here at Neatono's last exclamation," I said. "For biological entities such as ourselves, we believe reality is what we are experiencing. But is it not also true that our sensory equipment is not only limited in its ability to sense the entire range of attributes of physical reality, but, indeed, it can be faulty as well?"

"Quite so," remarked Neatono. "Our eyes work well within the range of what we call visible light, but we know that this is but a minuscule fraction of the wavelengths of light that permeate the universe. This shows the limited range of our sense of sight, and, parenthetically, in a real-world example, I'm sorry to tell you that I suffer from cataracts, and my vision is the poorer for it. Colors fade, vision blurs, and in bright sunlight a cloudy haze obscures much before me. An already limited sensory organ has become even more so with age and disease."

"I am sorry to hear that," I said, "and I hope you will see an ophthalmologist to have that corrected, as the surgery is very successful these days."

"I do have a surgery date," he said, "and am sorry I have waited so long to do so, but the surgery scares me nonetheless, as I imagine the worst outcome as opposed to the best."

"Fear not, my friend," I replied, "for I'm sure it will be a great success. Rest assured, I am available to give you a hand, as are your sons as well."

"I thank you for your offer and your kindness," he said.

"So as I was saying," I continued, "not only is our sight sense limited in terms of wavelength and malfunction, but the organs of sight limit the size of the objects we can discern. A whole universe of microscopic organisms and particles exists below this threshold.

"So our experience of reality is an interpretation by our central nervous system, with the only access we have to that reality being our sensory inputs. And if the stimuli from those inputs are not the same thing as the attributes of reality they are sensing, then time being a part of that reality will also be an interpretation created by our central nervous system and not the thing itself."

"It follows," said Neatono.

"And how can we describe this experience of time?" I asked.

"Well, as we would all agree," said Neatono, "time moves from an unknown future through a present now moment and immediately into an unchanging, and, as far as we know, unchangeable past."

"I think we can all agree on that, Father," said Ankistro.

"So would you agree that the only actual part of the time sequence we actually experience is the present or now moment?" I asked.

"That would seem to be the case," said Neatono. "The past we can only access as memories, which is itself a biochemical process, and the future is not yet manifest, though we may anticipate it, which is also a biochemical process."

"Quite right," I replied. "And these and all biochemical processes occur in this now moment of time. It is where we continually find ourselves as the seconds tick by."

"So what are you saying?" asked Miapetra. "Do the future and past not exist except in our minds?"

"What I'm getting at," I replied, "is that the only place in time that we seem to have actual access to reality is in this now moment we call the present. This seems to be the only place in our experience of time where we might say the organism is in sync with reality, but this is not so. Everything about the sensory input loop conspires to keep the organism out of sync with actual reality. Described simply, it takes a discrete amount of time for the impulses from our sensory system to reach the brain for processing and a discrete amount of time for the processing and experiencing of the unfolding events. What we experience as now has already happened. The 'now' experience of the organism is part and parcel of the actual biochemical process of stimulus interpretation and representation."

"Hmmmm," said Sanida, "things sure seem to happen in the present; when I rub my eyes or scratch my arm, I feel it now, and it seems as real as anything."

"We cannot transcend this biological system, which interfaces with reality, to create our experience of reality," I said. "As mentioned before, it works beautifully to keep us alive and seamlessly interfacing with the world. And it is self-correcting, because if it did not work, we would be extinct and would not be having these experiences at all!"

"Hmmmm," continued Sanida.

"Let's take a deeper cut on the experience of this now moment we find ourselves in," I said.

"As we know, light's speed, though constant and fast, is not instantaneous. The farther away objects and events are from us, the longer it takes that information to reach our senses. Everything we experience as happening now has already transpired, yet we experience the world as a now moment, moving from future to past, and containing events that occur simultaneously. No matter how hard we try, we can never partake of an actual now moment. The best we can do is hone our sensory system to operate at its peak efficiency and speed to close the gap between how much and what we experience as a now moment and what actually happened."

Neatono said, "On this point, you are absolutely correct. The physics is clear on the matter, and so it seems that our biological representation of the present now moment is an experience that is inaccurate at best."

"Just so," I replied.

"Well," said Geraki, "it may be that our interpretation and representation of the world may be necessarily inaccurate by design, but that doesn't mean that time does not have an arrow. The effects of time are all around us—aging parents, erosion—and entropy itself seems proof enough of its reality."

"The matter and forces of the universe do not 'experience' anything," I said. "They simply are. Biological observers experience and categorize things. To the elements, there is no big or small, simply a range of scales. There is no hot or cold, simply a range of temperatures. There is no red or blue, simply a range of wavelengths. There is no up or down, left or right, simply points in space. Any qualities that appear to exist in any of these attributes are created by our biology, and they seem real enough to us. But now that we see that time itself is also part of this interpretation of reality, we have to ask ourselves whether there is really a past or future, or if they are simply points in time."

"It is just so difficult to conceptualize such a reality," said Neatono. "Even though you make a convincing case that our experience of time is really an interpretation, I think that that idea is imaginary, and my experience is actually real."

"Well," I said, "let's try using a metaphor much as Brian Greene did with the loaf of bread to symbolize space-time."

"What will you devise?" asked Geraki.

"Let's imagine ourselves for a moment as blind fish," I said, "swimming in a vast expanse of water. We can feel something moving past us, but we don't know what. We can only feel and use the force of the water at the very position within it that we occupy. The experience of this fish is that the water it swam through is 'gone' and the water it's going to swim through does not yet exist to it, but its movement past the now experience of this water would be impossible, if the water did not exist as a whole."

"This metaphor does approximate what appears to be our own experience of time, while showing that the reality that the experience is based on is quite different," said Neatono.

"It is important to reiterate a distinction already made but that must be emphasized," I said. "The matter and forces of the universe do not 'experience' anything; they simply are. To experience something is to perceive it. The only things we know of in the universe that perceive are biological entities. They are platforms of perception and, as such, may be called observers. Manufactured interpretations of reality are unique to observers alone in the universe until the rocks or the stars begin to communicate and tell us otherwise.

"Transposing this metaphor to our situation," I said, "we can imagine that it is we, as observers, who are moving through the water, not the other way around. Likewise, we are blindly moving through a vast expanse of time, not the other way around. To move through it, it must be there already. Past, now, and future are our biologically created experience of moving through points in space-time that already exist."

"While your metaphor is convincing," said Geraki, "my experience of time and its arrow is still unshakable. I would like to believe, but I find I just can't make the leap."

I replied, "Admittedly, this metaphor, like most, is not perfect. We have to use our conception of time based on our experience of it to make sense of it. Indeed, it seems impossible for us to conceptualize any property of time that does not include its movement."

Neatono began leafing through one of the many books lying on the table next to his chair. Finally, landing on a particular page, he said, "I remember Stephen Hawking's discussion of the arrow of time in his book *A Brief History of Time* and took it at face value. But what you say may cast it in a new light, for it shows just how difficult it is to break the bonds of the belief that our experience of time is the reality of time itself. Here, let me quote to you from the book:

When one tried to unify gravity with quantum mechanics, one had to introduce the idea of "imaginary" time. Imaginary time is indistinguishable from directions in space. If one can go forward in imaginary time, one ought to be able to turn round and go backward. This means that there can be no important difference between the forward and backward directions of imaginary time. On the other hand, when one looks at "real" time, there's a very big difference between the forward and backward directions, as we all know. Where does this difference between the past and the future come from? Why do we remember the past but not the future?

"Indeed," I said, "this passage highlights his assumption that our biological experience of time is 'real,' and he is attempting to reconcile it somehow with the physics where 'imaginary' time plays an important role, and one ought to be able to move backward or forward in it as easily as in space. Even Stephen Hawking can't break the grip of our biologically created experience of the arrow of time as being real," I said.

"The same can be said of the memories he's talking about," said Neatono. "If we look through the lens of an observer of biological experience, we see that memories of the past are simply biochemical processes, which is all our biology will allow us to create. We also have experiences of the unknown future in the sense of anticipatory feelings and thoughts, and these are also biochemical processes. These memories have the same relationship to real points in space-time as the experience 'heat' does to an actual physical attribute of temperature in reality; they are interpretations and not the things themselves."

"This is true," I said, "and an important point to remember, as we move forward in our exploration."

SIX

"I am still unwilling to give up my belief in time with its arrow," said Miapetra, "but I am willing to continue this exploration into the nature of time and space and whether my experience is illusory or not."

"I too cannot give up my commonsense notion of time, as I experience it," said Oachyronas, joining in. "There are just too many strange outcomes, if what you are proposing is true. For instance, if all time exists then from our biological vantage point, that means that the future already exists, yet I can't experience it. I know tomorrow will come, but I know not what it brings, whereas if the future does indeed exist, I should be able to experience it."

"So if I were to ask you, Oachyronas, what any particular point in space means, could you give me an answer?" I asked.

"I could tell you the position of such a point, which is simply a fact, but as to its meaning, it would have none," he replied.

"And if there were a large stone in that point in space, would that qualify to give the point meaning?" I continued.

"I would say no. I could describe the stone and place it in space, but it has no meaning," he said.

"And what would it mean if the stone and your foot both shared the same point in space?" I asked.

"That would mean that my foot was most probably damaged, and I in pain," he replied. "I would either remove my foot or the stone from that point in space."

"Then would you agree that meaning is intrinsic to conscious observers, as we've defined them, but is not present in inanimate objects?" I asked.

"It would certainly seem that way," he said. "I can't think of a situation where mere facts, outside of the purview of a conscious observer, would have any meaning," he replied.

"And would you agree that, in the same situation, where the rock and your foot shared the same point in space, there is still no meaning with respect to the rock and its position in space, whether or not your foot is there?" I asked. "That the rock has no desire to harm you or to move from that place, so that the meaning is for you and you alone?"

"Upon reflection, I would have to agree," he said.

"So whatever meaning you may create out of the possible facts regarding the nature of time in the universe, that nature will not be affected. Indeed, you may deny the facts most vociferously, but the facts themselves will remain unchanged," I said.

The room grew quiet after this last exchange. After a moment, I began again.

"Einstein has shown that the now of one observer may be in the past or future of another observer by dint of their relative movement through space-time. There is no discernible overarching now moment in the universe that all others are measured against. In their great proliferation, all are relative. The gamut of reference frames that permeate space-time make a mockery of time's arrow. Without a universal now, how can we speak of a meaningful arrow of time other than one created by an observer?

"The great problem we need to overcome is that we have no words to help us form a conceptual framework within which time, without a now, is ever present in the universe. Whenever we try, our words, based on our experience, drag us back to our familiar ways of thinking, and when we try to describe time without its familiar arrow, we use words that describe or imply its movement nonetheless.

"I would like to shift our focus to a place in physics where the multiple now moments of relativity seem tame in comparison, namely to the discipline of quantum mechanics," I said.

SEVEN

"How many of you are familiar with quantum mechanics and its elements?" I asked.

"I have studied the basics of the subject," said Sanida.

"I have also studied it with respect to its information regarding time," said Neatono.

"Good," I said. "Have the rest of you heard of it?" I asked.

They had all heard of it, but they knew no details of the subject.

"What you will hear may sound like science fiction, but I can assure you the results are tested and represent the way things actually seem to work in reality," I said.

"Even in relativity we speak of a before and after, even if we can't agree on exactly when those points in time exist. In the quantum world, things are not so simple," I said.

"I think I'll open some more wine for this," said Nikitis. "Sounds like we're going to need it."

"That's fine," I said, "but keep your wits about you. You're going to need them, if you wish to follow this line.

"I don't want to get into the history of the development of quantum mechanics as that subject alone is a semester course at university. Let me just describe the basic elements of the subject. Firstly, QM, the shorthand for quantum mechanics, studies nature at the smallest levels—that is, at the atomic and subatomic levels."

"What I find most interesting," said Neatono, "is that relativity and QM both describe, with great accuracy, the workings of the natural world. Yet they are incompatible inasmuch as relativity is relevant to large macroscopic systems like planets, stars, and galaxies, and QM relates to microscopic systems on the level of the Planck length—that is, the level of atoms and smaller."

"That is correct," I said. "Two theories of one universe that don't play together very well in each other's yard. But to get back to a description, the quantum in quantum mechanics describes the fact that the physical properties of the universe, like energy or charge, appear in discrete units, or quanta."

"Can you give us a real-world example of that?" asked Oachyronas.

"Imagine that in my gym I do three things. I sit on a stool, I walk on a treadmill, and I sprint on a stationary bicycle. Each activity represents a higher level of energy. That is, sitting is base level, walking is next, and sprinting is the highest. In classical mechanics, also known as CM, it was believed that the change in energy states was smooth and continuous. My energy state would slowly rise from sitting to walking, over time to the maximum level at walking, and then the same from walking to sprinting. QM has shown that this is not how energy moves through systems. Instead, the sitting energy level remains at one fixed level and does not change. In order to move to the walking energy state, I must absorb a discrete packet or quanta of energy. At the moment I absorb this quanta of energy, I immediately change my position from sitting to walking. There are no other values to the energy states between the two different quantum states of energy. Also, the transformation occurs instantaneously. The same is true for walking to sprinting. To move back down the energy ladder, I would give up a quanta of energy and move instantaneously to the next lower level. Does this make sense?" I asked.

"I can't say it makes sense, but I understand what you are saying. And QM has shown that this is the way the universe works at these atomic levels?" he asked.

"QM is considered the most accurate theory ever devised, and its incredibly accurate predictions have been shown to be the way the universe works at the subatomic level, though larger systems, into the molecular size, have been shown to follow QM's laws.

"Another important aspect of QM is the wave-particle duality of all matter and energy. At the subatomic level, all objects exhibit both wavelike and particle-like aspects, depending on how they're being measured, meaning observed. I'll get more into this in a moment. And finally, for our purposes, there is the Heisenberg uncertainty principle, which turns QM into a purely probabilistic theory. Unlike CM, in QM nothing about any observed particle can be known with one hundred percent certainty."

"In school, we touched briefly on QM," said Sanida, "and it sounded more like magic than reality, except the experimental proof was incontestable."

"Quite so," I said, "and Einstein, who brought us relativity, was an important contributor to QM in its early days and was given a Nobel Prize for his discovery of the photoelectric effect, which is a QM phenomenon. He, however, became disenchanted with the theory, because, as he famously said, 'God does not play dice,' meaning the probabilistic nature of the theory was a flaw to his mind, and he believed there was some hidden variable that QM simply hadn't discovered yet."

"As I remember, it was this uncertainty principle that was causing all the consternation, wasn't it?" asked Neatono.

"Very much so," I replied, "and Einstein tried to show that it was based on an incomplete knowledge of reality and would disappear when the unknown piece of the puzzle was finally found. This was something he spent the rest of his life trying to reconcile with his work on the GUT, or grand unified theory, also known as the theory of everything."

"While everything you've described thus far is pretty strange, I have a feeling there is something much stranger you are going to reveal," said Oachyronas.

"True indeed," I said, "and it has to do with a physicist named Thomas Young. Young's experiment, also known as the double-slit experiment, contains the only mystery in QM, according to the great physicist Richard Feynman, and exemplifies the wave-particle duality of nature in unambiguous terms. Young took a metal plate with two slits in it and placed it in front of a detector screen to mark the impacts of the photons passing through the slits. When shining a beam of light at the plate, the pattern that was revealed on the impact detector screen showed a wave interference pattern."

"As I remember learning," interrupted Neatono, "CM considered light to be corpuscular—that is, like tiny balls—but the evidence that light could be made of waves was a troubling problem. Young's experiment proved once and for all that light exhibited wavelike properties, because, if light were corpuscular, there would be two lines of impacts on the impact detector screen, relating to the two slits. Instead, a pattern of light and dark bands was revealed, a classic wave interference pattern for this type of experiment."

"Then how did it show the corpuscular quality of light?" asked Oachyronas.

"That is the most interesting outcome of the experiment," I said. "Firstly, the impact detector screen revealed the light as corpuscular entities—that is, discrete dots—while the pattern itself was a classical wave interference pattern. It might be noted here that objects as large as 180 atoms will exhibit some form of wave function in this experiment, but the usual objects are light, electrons, and atoms."

"Couldn't the light particles or electrons or whatever somehow be interfering with each other as they go through the slits?" asked Oachyronas.

"Good question—and one they asked themselves," I replied. "In fact, they tried firing single photos—that is, one photon at a time at the slits. Wouldn't you know it? The pattern that slowly emerged was a wave interference pattern. There was also absolutely no way to determine beforehand where the particle would land. That information could only be a probabilistic one. Eventually the experiment was run using other detectors set up at the slits to determine which slit the photons were going through. When one photon at a time was fired at the slits without these detectors, the pattern that developed on the impact detector screen was a wave interference pattern. Then, when these detectors were used to determine which slit any single photon went through, the pattern on the impact detector screen was a classic particle pattern, where two rows of impacts correlated to the two slits in the plate. The mere act of observing which slit the photon went through changed the particle's characteristic from wavelike to particle-like."

"You mean to say that just the act of observing the particle will change its character and make it act one way as opposed to another?" asked Oachyronas.

"That is what the experiments showed," I said. "Not only that, but the physicist John Wheeler, who was very interested in these results, developed an ingenious variant on the experiment that he called the delayed choice experiment. The choice in this experiment was either to look at which slit the particle went through or not to look. The setup of this experiment allowed experimenters to change which experiment was being done after the emitted particle had already 'made the choice' of which slit to go through. Successfully completed, these experiments seemed to show that the type of measurement itself, observed or unobserved, is determining 'after the fact' which route the particle will have traveled."

"Let me see if I understand this," said Sanida. "The experiment would send particles through the double-slit plate and determine which slit they went through, which should make them act like particles. Then they could erase that information, after the fact but before the particles reached the impact detector screen, so that the experimenters once again wouldn't know which slit they had gone through, and the electrons would behave like waves again?"

"That is correct," I said. "Additionally, they could fudge the erasure so that, say, fifty percent of the time they'd know which slit the particle went through, and the pattern on the detector screen would show a mix of fifty percent classic particles and fifty percent wave-interference pattern."

"Wow," said the assembled. "Unbelievable."

"And this is the way the world really works?" asked Oachyronas.

"Let's just say that these results are observed every time this experiment is run," I replied.

"But what does this all mean?" asked Oachyronas.

"Remember what we discovered the last time you asked the meaning of the physical properties of the universe we live in," I said. "The point is that the world as we experience it every day and the actual properties of that world do not exactly correlate. What we are looking to discover is whether there is a dissonance between our experience of time and the nature of time as it is in reality."

"So do you mean to say that no one has asked what these strange results mean with regard to our everyday experience of the world?" he asked.

"There are numerous attempts to explain QM's results, but, for the most part, they read more like religious texts than physics texts," I explained. "The Copenhagen interpretation says that there is no objective reality behind the formalism of QM. There is really nothing more to say about it than that we make the measurements we make, and the results comport with our predictions—end of story. There is the many-worlds interpretation that says that every quantum choice splits the universe in two such that another universe appears in order to account for the two choices available to the system. Each universe goes along its merry way, each splitting ad infinitum. There's also a transactional interpretation that requires wave probability functions to travel back in time as well as forward, and there are others as well, but, as you can see, it's a sticky wicket," I said.

"Well, Socrates, I'm sure you must have something to say on the subject since you've seen well enough to bring us to this point," he said.

"What I'd like to highlight at this point," I said, "is the connection between observation and the resulting QM conundrums. All these results assume that the observer's observations, though they seem to affect the results of these experiments, are on par with reality itself. If you remember, we have already shown that the only observers we know of are ourselves, biological entities whose interpretations of reality are not reality itself. We have also seen other QM results where time is involved in abnormal ways, the instantaneous shifting of quantum energy states by electrons where delta T, meaning a change in time, equals 0, as well as the change in the state of particles after the fact in the delayed choice experiments, whereby it appears that the particles are in an abnormal relationship with time. All these results are interpreted according to a conscious now moment through which particles come and go, a now moment we've discovered is arbitrary and relative."

"So tell us, Socrates, is there a way out of this labyrinth?" asked Neatono.

"Before we can answer that," I said, "we need to look at another vexing problem that was raised by QM. As mentioned earlier, Einstein was having serious problems with quantum mechanics and its implications, believing that some vital information was missing from the theory because 'God does not play dice.' To hopefully prove QM incomplete, Einstein, along with Boris Podolsky and Nathan Rosen, created a thought experiment, now called the EPR experiment, after the initials of their combined last names, to show the incompleteness of QM, using the paradox of entangled particles."

"And what exactly are entangled particles?" asked Oachyronas.

"These are two or more particles that are 'subsets' of a larger quantum entity that must follow the probabilistic rules of QM as if they are one particle," I replied. "The problem is that QM entangled particles—let's say polarized photons—flying off in different directions at the speed of light, share a single quantum state. The uncertainty principle tells us that one can never know certain complementary variables such as momentum and position with one hundred percent accuracy. With entangled particles such as these photons, I'd have a fifty percent chance of measuring polarization plus Z in the Z direction, but should I make that measurement and find a plus Z then someone measuring the partner particle would find a minus Z polarization with one hundred percent accuracy no matter how far apart the particles were. A measurement here would mean an instant state change somewhere else. How does the partner particle 'know' what state to be in? This went against Einstein's ideas of 'locality,' meaning there is no information that can travel faster than light, and 'realism,' meaning if I'm not looking at the moon, that doesn't mean it's not there. EPR thought they'd created an insurmountable obstacle for QM to overcome, but, in 1964, John Bell, using the EPR reasoning, showed that a choice of measurement setting here shouldn't affect the outcome there and vice versa. This is known as Bell's theorem or Bell's inequality. In 1972, it was used to show that the predictions of QM are correct and 'nonlocality,' or what Einstein called 'spooky action at a distance,' is real; quantum-entangled particles communicate state instantaneously, at any distance. Once Bell's inequality was breached, the EPR experiment showed that there were no hidden variables; communication of the particles' states were occurring between the particles over any distance instantaneously."

"So, two theories, relativity and QM, contradict each other—so what? Theories are, after all, well, theories. They're not reality, are they?" Neatono asked.

"Both of these theories," I said, "make predictions about the extraordinary reality of the universe that have been shown to be extremely precise. Relativity's construct of space-time and the inviolability of the speed of light, the effects on time and objects in space-time, depending on the relative motion of observers, and the effects on time of gravitational fields, the bending of light by gravitation. These effects were theorized, quantified, and proven to be as proposed. QM's predictions are, likewise, validated by empirical evidence, and the phenomena they embody, such as particles that can occupy more than one space at the same time, entanglement and nonlocality, wave-particle duality, and the uncertainty principle are vital to modern electronics and chemistry, to name two fields. We see two things that seem irreconcilable and yet appear real. Is there another phenomenon in human experience we can point to with similar properties?" I asked.

EIGHT

"Socrates," said Sanida, "I think I see where you're heading with this. From a physiological point of view, we call such phenomena optical illusions, which are well studied and have similar properties—that is, observed results that are irreconcilable. Such illusions include the 'contingent perceptual aftereffect,' the 'blind spot,' 'afterimages,' 'contrast and color illusions,' and more."

"And how are these optical illusions created?" I asked.

"They are the products of an experience that is interpreted incorrectly because of the structure or fault of the sense apparatus and/or the central nervous system itself," he said.

"And would you agree that while the optical form of these illusions are the best studied, all the senses would fall under the same type of influence?" I asked. "That is, that they are fallible and prone to reporting erroneous information, because they are interpretive mechanisms that are not reality itself?"

"I would agree with that point," he said, "because, as you've described already, the central nervous system creates its representation of reality from a discrete set of sensory inputs, which are limited in the type of signal they provide, are prone to damage and inaccuracy, and, most importantly, are not reality itself."

"And let me ask this," I said. "If we are aware of an illusion and have studied its causes, could we classify it as an imperfect illusion because we know the difference between the illusion's effects and the reality of what we're experiencing, even if the illusion persists in the experience?"

"I think that would be a reasonable classification," replied Sanida.

"Then couldn't there also be a class of illusion we might call perfect illusions, because we have no idea they are illusions? So that without an understanding that a certain experience is actually an illusion, we accept it as real," I said.

"How do you mean, Socrates?" Sanida asked. "Can you give an example?"

"I cannot give an example of a perfect illusion, because, by definition, we believe the experience to be real," I said. "However, I think I can approximate something similar."

"Please enlighten us," said Sanida.

"There is a well-known phenomenon called 'false memory,' which actually occurs in all people," I began. "Though the causes of false memory formation are only now being understood, their effects are very real and cover such experiences as witnessing someone commit a crime when that person did not, witnessing erroneous events at an accident, and remembering events one has participated in without ever having been at the place the events occurred. In fact, even remembering having committed a crime oneself when one never did, can occur. To all intents and purposes, these memories are absolutely real to the rememberers and reflect experiences they absolutely believe they had. To try to refute them is a very difficult undertaking, sometimes even impossible. People have done jail time and even been executed based on someone's false memories. Additionally, false memories can affect larger groups of people and whole communities such as in the Salem witch trials and the McMartin preschool sexual abuse cases. The only reason we can't classify these as 'perfect' illusions is that we now know they were illusions. So from them we can surmise that perfect illusions exist and that they have real-world effects for the observers and those around them."

"So you're saying that in the case of 'perfect' illusions, there can be no distinction made between the illusion and reality—that the proposed illusion is taken as reality itself?" Sanida asked.

"That would be an effect of this classification of sensory illusion," I replied.

"This sounds crazy though," said Miapetra. "These effects of relativity and QM are very real. Surely you're not saying they are illusions."

"I do not wish to confuse us by making such a judgment," I replied, "but history has shown us that humanity has lived with many perfect illusions based on the experiences of their day. I think you yourself could give some examples if you tried."

"Hmmmm," he said, "let's see, flat earth; geocentricism; the four humors: blood, yellow bile, black bile, and phlegm; and the four elements theory of matter. Yes, I see your point."

"As perfect illusions, these experiences were 'facts' that were 'real' to those in their day, indistinguishable from reality itself," I said. "And, at the time, these populations believed that they were at the forefront of knowledge of the universe. These perfect illusions brought real 'advancements' to culture, arts, sciences, and politics. History shows us a long line of generations of humans being at the forefront of knowledge, bringing new advances along with them. Is it possible to say now that we are at the apex of knowledge—that what we now know is truly real?" I asked.

"Um—" began Sanida.

"But this is not a discussion I wish to continue," I interrupted. "Rather, I simply wish to ascertain the acceptance of a classification of illusion we can call 'perfect,' whose attributes are that the illusion both exists and yet is indistinguishable from what we experience as reality itself due to the organism's biochemical nature and its dependence on its interpretation of reality," I said.

"I think you have made your point, and it is a sobering one," replied Sanida.

"And what of theatrical illusions, the type one sees at magic shows?" asked Miapetra.

"Those would fall under the classification of imperfect, as the causes of the illusions, though manipulated by persons to fool the sensory system, are known and knowable," I replied.

"But this does bring up another class of illusions, whose existence lends great evidence to the biochemically manufactured nature of experienced reality, and it is the class exemplified by dreams," I said.

"You never cease to surprise me," said Sanida. "In the way you have defined illusions, I would have to agree that dreams would fall into another class indeed."

"And, as a class, they are remarkable in their ability to create in the sleeping organism a complete and extraordinary reality that Carl Jung called 'realer than real,'" I said. "In fact, many ancient, and even modern, peoples view the dream state as another deeper or holier reality than waking reality," I said.

"The dreaming organism is all the evidence we would need to show the role of the central nervous system in the production of an experience of reality, in this case from whole cloth," said Sanida.

"All the senses are involved in dream experiences, and the reality produced is, well, unreal in its representation, as they include experiences like flying, breathing underwater, being younger or older, or of a different sex," I said. "We see colors, we taste, and we feel—the entire gamut of sense perception is in play—yet the sensory system lay with the body in a bed asleep. I would like to call this the 'creative' illusion because of its dramatic and almost theatrical nature."

"This seems an appropriate name for the phenomenon," said Sanida.

"We could categorize yet other forms of illusion if we wished, such as the reality manufactured by diseased or malformed sensory apparatus, or reality manufactured under environmental or physical duress. But, yet again, this could be a complete university seminar and would be a digression from our current course," I said.

"So at this point in our discussion, I propose to state the following, and see if you agree."

"Proceed," said Sanida.

"That human experience is an interpretation of actual reality by the central nervous system. This is accomplished using the biochemical and biomechanics tools of the organism to report attributes of actual reality via stimulus to the central nervous system. This experience is not actual reality itself.

"That this human experience is prone to inaccuracies and inconsistencies in its representation of reality due to the limitations and imperfections of the sense apparatus and/or the central nervous system itself, and exhibits these imperfections in phenomena we shall call illusions.

"That there are at least three classes of illusions, the first being 'imperfect,' because we know the difference between the illusion's effects and the reality of what we're experiencing, even if the illusion persists in the experience. Such illusions are usually the result of 'hardwiring' issues that result in effects like 'afterimage' reported by the retina to the brain, among others.

"The second being 'perfect,' such that the illusion both exists and yet is indistinguishable to the organism from reality itself because of the organism's biochemical nature and its reliance on an interpretation of reality created without vital input it lacks access to. Such illusions persist until empirical evidence proves them otherwise, and even then the organism may still not accept the experience as an illusion.

"The third being 'creative,' in which the organism's central nervous system creates from whole cloth alternative experiences of reality irrespective of sensory input. This product, no matter how phantasmagorical, corresponds to the organism's sensory input structures, an example being dreams."

Putting this forward, the assembled group, with some mumbling and nodding, agreed with the propositions.

"So we have experiences based in biochemical processes that relate in one way or another to what we call reality and that we believe faithfully represent that reality, but we also agree that neither these processes themselves nor their product are that actual reality," I said.

"And we have shown that there is a class of experiences called illusions, which are poor to false representations of what we call reality, and that they are so with respect to the experiences just mentioned," I said. "Would you agree with this?"

"Yes," replied Sanida. "The illusions are obviously an inferior form of a representation of reality compared with the superior form they come from."

"And what form would this superior form be?" I asked.

"It would be the system in place that is part and parcel of the proper functioning for the organism itself," he replied.

"So you are saying that there is an optimal system of sensory interface and interpretation that is part and parcel of the design of the organism?" I asked.

"There would have to be," he said.

"And let us imagine that, of an entire population, one individual possessed the most perfect system of sensory interface and interpretation that the species could create," I said. "Could we call this a 'prime' system, that is, the system by which all others could be measured in terms of the optimum level of their functioning?" I asked.

"I think that would be useful," said Sanida, "given we need some biological and biochemical interpretive system to compare the illusory interpretations to."

"And would you agree," I continued, "that even though this prime system operates at an optimum level, it is still nonetheless a system that interprets received stimuli to create an experience of reality for the organism?"

"We have already agreed to this premise," said Sanida.

"That is true," I replied, "but in the context of illusory experiences, we need to clarify that though they are poor to false representations compared with what would be their prime experience, the prime experience itself would also not be reality, but yet another biologically created experience of reality."

"Yes," replied Sanida, "but the prime system is a truer interpretation of reality than the illusory ones."

"Truer to what?" I asked.

"Truer to actual reality," he replied.

"Have you heard the saying 'bread is the staff of life'?" I asked.

"Yes," he replied, "though I have moved to a gluten-free diet since the onset of some arthritis, and it appears to be helping."

"I'm glad to hear it," I said, "for I too have developed arthritis in my hands and know the discomfort of its constant pain. Perhaps I'll try the gluten-free option myself and see how it works."

"That is a good idea," he said, "but we digress. Yes, I have heard the saying, as I'm sure everyone here has."

All nodded.

"So would you agree that its meaning implies a connection between bread and life itself?" I asked.

All nodded again.

"Then let's pretend that you still eat bread, and I know some of you do," I continued. "If I were to give you a slice of my own homemade product, and you discovered a strong yeasty taste not to your liking, or a dense and crumbly texture unfit for sandwiches, or a too-sweet taste due to a surfeit of sugar, or too gluey, or too dry—this offering, though unpleasant and not up to the standards of what you consider to be an acceptable approximation of what good bread should be, would still be considered a bread product by dint of the process by which it was created. Would you agree?" I asked.

"Though upon tasting I might proclaim that 'this is not bread,' I see what you mean. My proclamation would reflect my opinion that the offering was not up to my standards, but that does not change the process by which the product was made, namely the process of bread making," Sanida said.

"Then you will agree that these so-called inferior products are still bread products, and that their inferiority does not infer that the product we would compare them to is of a different nature—that, in fact, all these products use the same production process, and so all are of the same nature, namely bread?" I asked.

"I agree," he said.

"And will you further agree that, though we can compare one judged variety of bread against another and find one agreeable and another disagreeable, we cannot claim for the agreeable product a nature other than its own. In other words, we cannot claim that because we like the one bread over all others it is the closest to life or nature or any other essence other than its own," I said.

"Only through hyperbole, for though we like it more, it is still bread by definition of the process by which it was created. We must agree with your statement," said Sanida.

"Then do you see that, with respect to the production of a biologically manufactured representation of reality by the central nervous system, there is no essential difference in the processes themselves between what we've termed illusory representations of reality and the prime system representation of reality?" I asked.

"I think we must agree with you on this point," said Sanida.

"Then like my poorly made bread, though we may not have an affinity for these representations of reality we call illusory, and though we may judge them to be unreliable or unreal, we do so against the only system of representation there is, of which the prime system along with all these others are like members."

"Once again we must concur," he said.

"We use the term *illusion* derogatorily as a judgment, comparing it to the prime system that we imbue with an essence it does not possess, namely a closer connection to reality. In fact, it is as removed from reality as are the illusory representations we've defined, and so either they may all be called illusory or we must rename them in some other way so as to reflect their familial essence," I said.

"The desire, no, but the need to feel that a particular experience of reality is closer to reality itself is overwhelming," said Sanida. "Even now, I want to cry out that what I am experiencing is real."

"You have hit the nail on the head," I said. "If we continue with this moment of self-reflection, we hopefully have noticed during our conversation about illusions that it was easy to accept their existence if we were involuntarily comparing them with an indelible inner image we all hold of true reality. But where does this image come from? We then defined a prime system of biochemical representation of reality; it would be the only system that could supply such an inner image. But as we have seen, it creates experiences of reality in the same way the so-called illusions do; they are all in the same family. Until we understand that everything we experience is akin to these illusionary experiences, we will be unable to peer past the curtain these illusions throw before us and so lose all hope of glimpsing something truly real."

NINE

"Socrates," said Neatono, "our minds are reeling, and the very ground we think we stand on shifts beneath our feet."

"I am glad to hear it," I replied, "for this is, I believe, the Zen experience of beginners' mind. In the experts' mind, few possibilities exist, but in the beginners' mind, there are many! We come to understand that our default system of knowing as an experience smothers any questions regarding its own veracity or the picture of reality it supplies. This is the shifting sand we feel beneath our feet and means, I think, that we are now ready to look at our universe with newly open minds."

"Is it worth taking such a journey?" asked Nikitis. "I was happy this morning when I knew that what I felt was real. How can thinking everything I experience is an illusion bring me peace or serenity?" he asked.

"The journey is not over," I replied, "but to maintain a lie when one has recognized it as such will not bring serenity I think."

"Perhaps," he said, "but I feel more like a hitchhiker who never bought a ticket for this journey. I fear for my sanity!"

"Fear not," I said, "for this truth has the power to turn the hitchhiker into the captain of his own vessel. Stay with us and have faith in the search for truth for, simply put, all else is not the truth."

"We are on this journey with you," said Neatono, "and we would be foolish to abandon it, so whence shall you lead now?"

"There is another thing that needs clarification before we can proceed to our original question of whether our experience of time is an accurate representation of the nature of time," I said.

"You have, thus far, shown us that our experience of reality is but an illusion. What more do you need to show us?" asked Neatono.

"To peer into the true nature of time is our goal. Let's see if we can get there now that we have the awareness of the illusory nature of our own experience of reality," I said. "But in order to continue, we need to look at yet another aspect of time that we take for granted."

"And what would that be, pray tell, as I hope you can shed some light on my own investigations," Neatono said.

"Perhaps I can," I said, "but it may not be what you expect."

"Then dally not," said Neatono, "but lead on."

"The question I have is this," I continued. "We not only experience an arrow of time, but the arrow of time we experience has a meter to it, seconds, minutes, hours, on and on. We take these to be real metrics of time's passage, but if our experience of time is illusory, then so are its metrics. Does anyone know how old we believe the universe we inhabit is?" I asked.

"According to the standard model, the universe began thirteen point seventy-four billion years ago," said Neatono.

"Very good," I said, "and when did you begin?" I asked.

"That would be seventy-four years ago," he answered.

"And how old is the earth?" I asked.

"We believe it to be around four billion years old," answered Neatono.

"And how long does the mayfly live?" I asked.

"Less than a day," replied Sanida.

"A day, and what is that?" I asked.

"One revolution of the earth on its axis," replied Miapetra.

"And can anyone find a standard metric of time's passage in all these examples?" I asked.

Silence filled the room. Finally, Neatono spoke. "There is nothing here we've defined that would rise to the level of an all-encompassing standard for time's passage—that is, a universal tick of the clock," he said. "Nor can I think of one."

"We know that there is no universal now from which all other nows can be compared," I said, "so are we surprised to find that there is no universal tick of the clock from which all other ticks can be measured?" I asked.

"That would be so," said Miapetra, "if the passage of time is part of the interpretation of reality created by our biology for our benefit."

"This could very well be the case," I said. "The only meaningful metric we can point to as being a tick of the clock on the axis of time's arrow is something we would have to define as delta T, but delta T does not measure a change in time at all. It measures a change in the state of some physical properties of the universe—say the change in position of a pointer on a round disk. In other words, time becomes measurable because we experience the universe in transformation through our now experience using an arbitrary measurement: delta T. There is no universal metric for the passage of time. The only thing we have that validates time's arrow is the experience of human observers."

"But we can measure these effects," said Miapetra. "You yourself have made reference to the accuracy of results postulated by relativity and QM."

"And so we finally come to it," I said. "This is one of those moments where one must use a thorn to remove a thorn. In order to arrive at this point, we have had no choice but to continue to use the results of experiments in our experienced reality. They are all we have with which to describe that reality. However, we now have the ability to shift our perspective whereby we can imagine that everything we have discovered about reality, and have been discussing, is based on our illusory experiences. The universe looks the way it does because our sensory and central nervous systems have created it to look just this way. This goes for all our experiments as well, for there are no experimental results without an observer. We can now say with some assurance that all these results are not an accurate depiction of reality at all."

"You are talking about anthropocentricism," said Sanida.

"Yes and no," I replied. "The usual meaning of the term relates to a prime experience of the universe and that Homo sapiens are the highest expression of nature, as are our perspectives and our accomplishments. I use the term very differently, and, though it still places Homo sapiens at the center of their universe, it debases the experience because of the limited access we have to reality through our central nervous system. The movement of time, the experience of a past, present, and future is a veil that covers the ultimate reality of the universe. In this case observing the universe with a past, present, and future can be compared to mistaking for reality the opaque surface of a hidden dimension."

"This is indeed a new view of humanity and our place in the universe," said Neatono. "This perspective though gives us the ability to use this limited biosensory system to imagine a reality it has no way of providing an experience of."

"In fact, from here on out we will have to differentiate the knowledge we 'know,' based on our viewing of it via this limited biosensory way, and a universe that may not comport at all with the experience of reality it provides," I said.

"We see the most contradictory and unbelievable results in our explorations of the universe via relativity and QM. Our scientists bend over backward to explain them in terms of our limited human observations, some claiming that the mere act of observation will determine which form, particle or wave, a quantum particle is, that observation itself dictates reality." I continued, "None other than John Wheeler, has claimed that human consciousness shapes not only the present but the past as well."

"These do seem like improbable explanations, but this is what we have found to be the way the universe works," said Neatono.

I replied, "Shall we say that the mere act of observation will determine which form, particle or wave, a quantum particle is, or can we also say that the mere act of observation will cloud the reality of a particle's nature and make it appear one way or the other?" I asked. "The same is true for Wheeler's belief that human consciousness determines reality, past and present, but it might also cloud reality itself by creating a past and present, which we believe is real but doesn't exist.

"The one and only common denominator in every experiment ever produced is a human observer, yet the act of observation, we've come to see, is an illusion whose foundation is the acceptance of a past, present, and future as real. We bend and twist the observations to make sense of the data as existing 'out there,' when in fact it's all 'in here,' in our biology and our sensory processing system."

"But what about all the proofs provided by amazing physics and mathematics?" asked Neatono.

"Scientists looking through the lens of human experience believe in the process of the universe becoming manifest in a now via an unknown future and into an unchanging past. The mathematics we have developed has become excellent at describing a universe that works in such a manner, but, if time does not flow, it is describing an illusion," I said.

"So you think all these scientists and the many theories out there are imaginary?" asked Neatono.

"A question has persisted since well before the time of the discovery of relativity, and it is this," I said. "Does the universe exist if we're not looking? I believe that the universe as we experience it does not exist when we're not looking, because we're actually creating it via our biology. A universe exists, but not this one of created human experience."

"So how can we possibly expect to discover this universe you believe exists outside of our experience?" asked Neatono.

"Because nature has shown her hand, but we've been unable to interpret it properly, dependent as we are on explaining all via our experience of it," I said.

"And what is this evidence nature has shown us?" Neatono asked.

"As we've experienced via QM, matter exhibits both wavelike and particle-like properties, and when we're caught observing them, they will exhibit one or the other, but we have no idea when or how they change state. The theory is that they exist in a superposition of both states, and, upon observation, their probability wave function collapses, and they become one or the other. Now Doctors S. Haroche and D. Wineland won the Nobel Prize in Physics in 2012 for actually creating particles in superposition. Doctor Wineland specifically created one electron that existed in two of its possible orbital positions simultaneously. How he did it is not the important point. That a particle is first in one place in space-time and then in two at the same time is a state change that occurs outside of time. This is not a particle moving to another place; it is a state change for a single particle. How long does it take for the particle to be in superposition? There is no now through which this transformation occurs. Without a now, there is no flow of time at all."

"But aren't these results explained by QM's theory and its mathematics?" asked Neatono.

"The same theory and mathematics created through the lens of our unshakable belief in the reality of time's arrow," I replied. "I suggest that this shows us another possibility."

"We are eagerly waiting to hear it," said Neatono.

"First we'll look at another phenomenon that will add some weight to this other possibility," I said. "In the case of quantum entanglement, Bell's inequality and subsequent experiments have shown communication between the particles over any distance occurs in delta T equals zero. Now in terms of state change, delta T equals zero defines not simultaneity but action outside of time, action in null time. There is no time lapse between superposition and probability wave function collapse. Theoretically, should the particles exist at opposite ends of the universe, communication exists over that span, which exists in null time. Some try to explain these results, but always through the lens of our experience of time. This is the universe that we experience when we're looking through the lens of time's arrow, so why don't we try imagining another universe that we've not looked at before."

"Too many now moments that don't agree, no now moments at all, time without a universal metric," said Neatono. "I am ready to remove this lens of flowing time from before my eyes and see something new."

"As with all illusory experiences, we will look to the thing that creates the wonder, which is also the thing that makes no sense," I said. "While the lack of a universal now or a universal metric for time indicates a divergence between our experience of time and its actual nature, the complete absence of a now moment in observed phenomena is one of those 'ignore that man behind the curtain' moments."

"How so?" asked Neatono.

"It defies everything our observational experimentation has shown us," I said. "It defies locality—the speed of light's speed limit for communication—and it defies reality itself. There is no explanation for it, and we accept it only because we must. We simply ignore this gorilla in the room and go about our business as if it weren't there. Because our observational experience of it is utterly and completely outside of everything we think we know about reality, it may be the piece of reality that pierces the veil of our illusion.

"If time does not have an arrow, if it does not flow at all but simply is, how could it have gotten that way?" I asked.

"The standard model says that everything in the universe was created in what is called the big bang, all matter, energy, space, and time," said Neatono. "Perhaps it was created at that moment."

"To speak of time being created in a moment makes no sense," I said. "If there was no time, there could be no moment. We continue to use our experience of time to try to explain time. There are, however, the observed phenomena of quantum super position and state changes. As we've seen, they occur, which is an inaccurate word to use, without a now, which is also an inaccurate description, but the only way we can describe it. What we can say is that without a now, anything can happen. A wave can become a particle. It can even go back in time to become a wave again. But remember, these are all phenomena we observe and experience as biological organisms via the lens provided by our sensory system. They are not reality itself."

"So how can we overcome this impasse?" asked Neatono.

"As a phenomenon that has broken through our illusions, it offers us a conception we can use. But as we know, these effects occur in the quantum realm of the subatomic world. This is why the phenomena of instantaneous communication of quantum-entangled particles over vast stretches of the universe are so important. Here are phenomena that unite the farthest reaches of the universe without a now moment. These quantum phenomena give us something to build with," I said.

"So how will you build with these phenomena?" asked Neatono.

"To speak of time's beginning is meaningless, but the phenomena of quantum superposition shows us a way. We can imagine that the entire universe appears in just such a superposition. There is no now within which it appears, yet it appears whole and complete, but not as we think we know it through our experience of it. Even now, I will have to use some of our conceptions of time to describe this, but it seems unavoidable at this point. Everything would seem to have appeared in delta T equals zero from our vantage point, from our experience. All matter, all energy, all space, and all time. From our vantage point, the beginning of the universe, the big bang, and the end of the universe—the big freeze or the big crunch—are separated by a vast ocean of time. Outside of our experience, the appearance of the universe, its so-called beginning and end are not separated at all, they appeared in null time, in delta T equals zero. Albert Einstein once said, 'The only reason for time is so that everything doesn't happen at once.' In fact, everything happens faster than that!"

"Are you saying that you believe the whole universe exists now—its beginning and end together?" asked Neatono.

"If the universe appears as a quantum object in superposition, to try to describe it as zero or null time is meaningless. Time did not exist, but, with its appearance, we cannot say time began—the best we can say is time is. I have to use our conceptions again, but the beginning and the end of the universe are connected, they appear together with everything else in the middle, though there is no middle either. This universe is one grand entangled particle in instantaneous contact with itself in delta T equals zero. Much like Schrödinger's famous cat, the universe both is, and is not, simultaneously. This is the meaning of IS outside of the observers purview."

"Well," said Neatono, "this is very difficult to wrap my mind around. You're saying that it's possible that all space, matter, and energy along with all time, even if it's an eternity of time, came into being in one fell swoop?"

"Something like that," I replied. "We have no way to know from whence the universe appeared, but the appearance of atemporal phenomena piercing through the veil of our illusion of temporality gives us reason to believe this is so. Our discussion began with the question of whether physics or our experience is wrong, given physicists' beliefs that time should not have an arrow, but that we experience it with one. How can we explain a universe where time has no arrow? I believe this is a way. But it also shows that the reality of this universe is far different from our experience of it."

"So what is this strange thing called the universe, as you're describing it?" he asked.

"The first thing to accept in this scenario," I said, "is that our concept of being is completely upended. Let's return to the conundrum of the double-slit experiment and especially John Wheeler's delayed choice variant. To Wheeler, the problem of the quantum is the problem of existence, of being. As Niels Bohr commented in a discussion with Heisenberg about the double-slit experiment, 'To be…to be…what does it mean to be?' regarding where *is* the particle? We are observing these particles behaving in ways that make no sense to our perception. Our experience of being requires an arrow of time, which is a creation of our biochemistry. It was, it is, and it will be. To biology, being is a now event. In the new universe, there is only IS, there is no was or will be."

"So in this new universe, time does not tick away at all; its function is quite different," said Neatono.

"Quite so," I said. "We must abandon this idea of the universe becoming something. Its beginning and its end are, but not in time as we experience it, so we can't say 'they are forever' or 'they have always been and always will be.' Being is not defined by time. Once we can conceptualize this, we can see that time acts more like pectin in a jelly; it is a solidifier. Far from being ephemeral and invisible, it acts to hold the universe together."

"So, if time is not flowing, then what are all these comings and goings, these births and deaths of stars and galaxies and people and civilizations?" asked Neatono.

"Neatono," I said, "we need a word that means 'being,' but outside of time, a complete being, which includes all the space, time, matter, and energy that comprise that being in this new universe. Do you have any suggestions?"

"Hmmm, what comes to mind is a blending of the Latin word for *complete* or *total*, which is *totus*, combined with *Is* to form *totIs* with a capital *I* in the *is* part of the word for clarity," he said. "The *tot* is pronounced like 'tote,' and the *s* in *Is* is more like a *z*, as in the word *is*."

"Good, good," I said. "I like it. So now if we wish to speak of the sun in our solar system but from the perspective of our new universe, we will make reference to our totIs sun, delineating its total being, including its entirety of birth and death. Let's see if this will help clarify our conceptualization of our totIs universe from our experience of our temporal universe.

"So back to your question," I continued. "In the totIs universe, where the dimension of time acts like a solidifier and is included in the totIs of all subsets of this universe, the comings and goings we experience in biology become like patterns and textures in its totIs, perhaps filaments and structural elements. We cannot experience the totIs of anything due to our biology, and so we're forced to use metaphors to try to describe it, but the main point is that nothing is becoming, everything IS in a totIs state," I said.

Suddenly, Miapetra asked, "Socrates, this has great bearing on what we were talking about earlier today. If, in a totIs universe, there is no past and no future, all just is, then probability disappears, and everything that will happen is known."

"Miapetra," I replied, "I'm afraid you've fallen into the trap of thinking of time in our well-worn way, while trying to imagine this new understanding. The totIs universe is aprobabilistic; there is no becoming or been. In the totIs universe, there simply is no probability. Einstein would like the totIs universe, because there is no 'spooky action at a distance' and no uncertainty principle."

"But I am sitting here with you, and I don't know what's going to happen tomorrow," he said.

"And you are convinced that this is reality," I said. "But it is biology and the experience of reality it gives you. Do you know of the Michelson Morley experiment?"

"I do." Chimed in Neatono. "Michelson and Morley were two scientists who, back in 1887, were looking to prove the existence of the 'luminiferous aether', or 'aether wind'—an as yet undetected substance thought to permeate the universe and which was believed to be the substance responsible for the propagation of light waves, much as water propagates water waves. As bodies moved through this aether it would appear as a 'wind' much like the wind we feel in a moving vehicle."

"That is correct." I said. "And their experiment ultimately disproved the existence of this 'aether.' This discovery was instrumental in the so called second revolution in physics that began a line of investigation leading to the special and general theories of relativity, thus changing forever our conceptions of space and time."

"And how does that relate to my not knowing what's going to happen tomorrow?" asked Miapetra.

"Because," I said, "our biologically created experience of times arrow may be, metaphorically speaking, this elusive aether. All the comings and goings brought about by flowing time that Neatono asked about earlier, exist via our biology's created aether of an arrow of time. It could never be detected 'out there' in the totIs universe, it only exists 'in here'; in the universe we experience as observers."

"Neatono," I asked. "Do you know how cosmologists view the creation and expansion of space in the standard model?"

"Yes," he replied, "very interesting and not at all an intuitive understanding."

"Please enlighten us," I said.

"Well," he began, "according to the standard model—which looks at the universe through the lens of flowing time— the universe is thirteen point seventy-four billion years old. It began from a singularity, conceptualized as a zero-point particle of infinite density and energy, and expanded from there. Contrary to what most people think, the big bang, or BB, was a moment of intense inflation of space-time that occurred shortly after creation and which, though brief, increased the size of the universe exponentially. Since then the universe has been expanding, not like an explosion where matter expands into existing space, but as space itself. Everything was created from the singularity and, to answer your question, space itself is expanding, but the most interesting facet of this expansion is that every point in space is the center of the universe—meaning that wherever an observer stands, all space around them is expanding away from that spot—because it all began from a singularity. The entire universe is a center, no matter where you are."

"Thank you, Neatono," I said, "well described. The salient point being that the standard model postulates a universe where every point is the center, even though we don't experience space that way. Space itself emerged from the singularity, or null point, and so no place can be considered a central point."

"And so something like this would be true of time as well in the totIs universe?" Neatono asked.

"Yes." I said. "Because if all time came to be in a quantum event, a universe appearing in superposition in null time—and let's not forget that a singularity, or zero point particle is a quantum entity—its beginning and its end exist together simultaneously. Like space in the standard model, there is no point in time in the totIs universe that can be considered a beginning or an end in time. In fact, there is no now at all."

TEN

"Anthropocentrism places human experience at the center of reality and distorts reality to comport with our experience of it. In the totIs universe our experience does not affect reality; our experience is a product meant for our own biology and nothing more. In discovering the qualities and ramifications of a totIs universe, we will have to relegate human experience to a minuscule subset of the totIs universe and try not to bend what we discover to accommodate our anthropomorphic neediness, which, I warn you, will be difficult," I said.

"So let's look at what some of these qualities and ramifications are," I continued. "First and foremost, time does not flow—it is."

"How can it flow if there is no now in the totIs universe?" asked Neatono.

"Exactly," I said. "And since time does not flow, the concept of moving backward, forward, or sideways through time is meaningless, the entire totIs universe simply IS."

"Can we measure time in the totIs universe?" asked Miapetra.

"Do we actually measure time in our universe?" I asked back.

"Well, we have clocks and all types of high-tech time pieces that seem to measure time," he said.

"Clocks and timepieces do not measure time," I replied. "They measure a change in state of some physical process, and we arbitrarily call that a passage of time. A swing of a certain pendulum we will call a second, some finite number of waves in the frequency of atomic movement we will call a nanosecond, and one revolution on Earth's axis we will call a day. We observe a physical process through a now moment, and we give it an arbitrary time signature, but actual time we have not seen nor measured."

"Then I imagine we won't be able to measure time in the totIs universe either," he said.

"Time cannot be measured in the totIs universe. Therefore, from our vantage point, the totIs universe is static, not dynamic. Time affords stability in the totIs universe, where we experience chaos and instability in ours," I said.

"Taken together, space and time form a structure more akin to a solid than the invisible aether we experience matter and energy operating within in our universe. It is an unchanging unity," I said.

"I know I asked before," said Miapetra, "but we see energy and matter moving through our universe, and you say the totIs universe is stable and solid. It is hard for me to conceptualize."

"Though space and time are more akin to a solid, they are not smooth and even. What we see in our biologically created experience as matter and energy interacting through space and in time are more akin to patterns and textures in the stable and static body of the totIs universe. Furthermore, because the totIs universe is static and stable, and there is no interaction of matter and energy through space and in time, the overall energy content of the totIs universe would be zero," I said.

"I have to ask," said Geraki, "if the totIs universe is real, why does it hide behind such an illusion and give us such an erroneous picture of itself?"

"My dear Geraki," I replied, "the totIs universe does no such thing. We, the creators of our experience of the totIs universe, observe these illusions that we create for ourselves. Because our very survival depends on trusting the experience of reality provided by our biology, it is impossible for us to give it up and believe it is illusory compared to the totIs universe. The totIs universe neither hides nor is hidden; we are simply unable to experience and observe it with the biology we have."

"You are right. I find it impossible to let go of my waking experience of the world as illusory, but I will try my best as you continue," he said.

"Thank you, Geraki," I said. "These are concepts that, though presented here this afternoon, will take some time to sink in and make any sense. Some rumination will be required and self-questioning as well.

"But let me ask you this, Geraki," I said. "What separates you and me?"

"Well, you are over there, and I am over here," he said.

"And when you say here and there, you are referring to points in space?" I asked.

"Yes, that is what I am referring to," he said.

"And how do you know that these points in space are separate?" I asked.

"Well, I cannot access your space from here. I would need to get up and walk over to be in your space and thus be connected to you," he said.

"And what have we learned of the measurement of time?" I asked.

"We do not actually measure time itself; we measure state changes in space using arbitrary delineation to represent time's passage," he said.

"Very good," I said. "And since time is measured by an observer, those physical state changes must occur through the observer's now moment for measurement," I said.

"Yes, that would have to be so," he replied.

"But in the totIs universe, we've seen that there is no now moment; all time appeared in no time at all, as did all space. In this scenario, there is no way to show that there is any separation anywhere between anything. Though it's putting it in our anthropomorphic way, everything in the totIs universe is connected to everything else. We can think of it as a very complicated quantum-entangled particle, or particles," I said.

"I don't mind being connected to some things," said Geraki, "but there are some things I definitely wouldn't want to be connected to."

"That is a true enough statement from a human perspective," I said, "but in the totIs universe, being is very different, and, thus, so are things."

"How so?" he asked.

"Well, once again," I said, "we observe separate things and interact with them in our universe, but the very definition of totIs excludes this. If we try to separate a totIs thing in the totIs universe, we have to include the entirety of its matter, energy, space, and time."

"So why can't I interact with a separate totIs thing?" he asked.

"Let's see who the totIs Geraki is," I said. "You would encompass your totIs from birth to death, in no time, but your birth is an arbitrary point in your totIs—would conception be a better point? I don't think so, your totIs is linked to your mother and father, and they to theirs in an unbroken line to the first living things whose totIs is connected to Earth itself."

"So in the totIs universe, I am connected to every living thing?" asked Geraki.

"And more," I said. "From our limited observational perspective, we want to be able to create subsets of our universe. But, in the totIs universe, there are no subsets, as the closer we try to find a boundary between things, the more the boundary smears out to connect with everything else."

"This is all fine and dandy," said Geraki, "but we're here in this universe, and I am here, but you're saying that in the totIs universe we are not here. We can't even find ourselves in that universe, so how can it be the real universe?" he asked.

"To answer that, we have to ask, 'Who are you?'" I replied. "Are you talking about the collection of atoms that make up your body, or are you talking about Geraki, the person with a unique personality and perspective of the world?" I asked.

"I think I'm talking about all of me," he said.

"Really?" I asked. "If Geraki were sleeping right now, could he be asking this question or even contemplating his place in the universe?"

"I guess not," he replied, "so it's I, Geraki, the unique personality, who I'm talking about."

"Then let's look at this again," I began. "Geraki, Socrates, Sanida—we are all observers of the universe. It is in the act of observation that we exist, and, if you remember, an observation is an experience of the universe. The process of observation and resultant experience requires a now moment through which we travel and is the platform from which we interact with the universe. But we have seen that even the prime system of biosensory processing and interpretation is akin to an illusion—the very process we use to experience and observe the universe. So who would you say you are?" I asked.

"So you are saying that we are just illusions?" asked Geraki.

"That would seem to be what I'm saying, but it is not accurate," I replied. "The totIs universe is—and we are—a part of this universe, so we are not an illusion per se. However, the nature of our experience and observation of the universe separates us from its true nature. I guess we could say that we are both real and an illusion together."

"Do you think there is any way for us to access the reality of the totIs universe as we are?" asked Neatono.

"To ask that question, we would have to ask ourselves who we would be if we could experience our totIs selves," I said. "Could we exist if we experienced our lives from birth to death in no time at all?" I asked. "The very nature of our unique being is nontotIs and requires the biochemical creation of an arrow of time for our existence. We cannot transcend the very process by which we exist, and so I do not believe it is possible."

ELEVEN

"So tell me, Socrates," asked Sanida, "if the totIs universe is complete and stable, encompassing all space and all time at once, wouldn't that mean, for us mere mortals, that everything has already happened?"

"Once again, meaning is a consequence of our being, not the universe's being. What does it mean to an atom or a snowflake if what you say is true?" I asked back.

"It seems pretty farfetched to believe that everything in the universe has already happened, to put it in human experiential terms. To imagine that everything that will happen tomorrow just on this little planet and just to humans, with all the decisions and coincidences leading to outcomes no one could have guessed, it just seems impossible, just too complicated to be reality," said Sanida.

"If we were on a golf course, and you were about to tee off on the eighteenth hole, and I asked you to indicate to me exactly which blades of grass were going to be affected by your golf ball on your drive, do you think you'd be able to do that?" I asked.

"Of course not," he replied. "The best I could do would be to come up with some kind of probability distribution curve that could give the probability of one of several outcomes," he replied. "Any attempt to discover such information is simply too complicated."

"So would you say that to come up with an answer of exactly which blades of grass will be affected by the ball is next to impossible?" I asked.

"Yes, I would say so," he replied.

"Yet when the ball is hit, it will affect very specific blades of grass and come to rest in a very specific place, will it not?" I asked.

"Indeed it will," he replied.

"Would you agree then that the seeming complexity and impossibility of predicting the outcome has no impact on the outcome itself?" I asked.

"That would seem to be the case," he said.

"And from whence comes such complexity and impossibility?" I asked.

"It comes from the inability to discern and compute the various environmental factors and the forces acting upon the ball," he said.

"And what is the source of this inability?" I asked.

"We do not have precise enough tools or a precise enough understanding to make such computations," he said.

"And what are these tools and understanding that stand in the way of making such computations?" I asked.

"The tools would allow us to make accurate measurements, and the understanding would allow us to use those measurements to come up with an answer to the problem," he replied.

"And would the tools, in and of themselves, be able to compute such an answer?" I asked.

"No, the various measurements would have to be analyzed by us, according to our understanding of the nature and workings of the various forces placed on the ball to determine such an outcome," he replied.

"So it is we, the observers, who are the source of the inability to compute such outcomes. Is that correct?" I asked.

"It would seem so," he replied.

"Then for whom or what does our inability to compute such outcomes have a bearing?" I asked. "In other words, is this inability a problem for us observers or for the totls universe?"

"Well it seems it would be a problem for both," he said.

"But you have already agreed that the seeming complexity and impossibility of predicting the outcome has no impact on the outcome itself," I said.

"Yes, that is true," he said.

"So if the totIs universe has no problem arriving at the exact answer to this question, then the problem would be ours," I said.

"So you have shown me," he said.

"Then I will say this: I believe the real problem you have with the unity of the totIs universe, its encompassing of all space and time from beginning to end, is not its complexity but its meaning for humanity with regard to free will, or the seeming loss thereof," I said.

"I admit that this thought is a worrying one for me, and I have been hoping that an answer would be revealed through our discussions," he said.

"And the same goes for me," said Neatono.

"And for all of us," the rest declared.

"By now it should appear clear to you," I said, "that problems we originally attributed to the universe are actually our own, like Sanida's issue with complexity."

"But the issue of free will cuts to the very heart of what it means to be alive and human," said Sanida.

"I will not argue with you there, Sanida," I said, "but it also lies at the very heart of why it seems impossible for us to accept that time does not have an arrow at all.

"The question of free will has concerned humanity from its earliest times, but I do not wish to explore the history of the freewill debate, as this record is not what concerns us here," I said.

"And what of the debate of the nature of free will itself?" asked Neatono. "Does this not have bearing on the subject of the totIs universe?"

"Can we all agree that the nature of the debate about free will essentially lies in the question of whether we humans have some or any control over our actions, and, if so, of what manner it is, and how much control can we actually exercise?" I asked.

"I think we can agree that you have posed the underlying question succinctly," said Neatono.

"Can we also agree that the very nature of the question of free will is intimately related to our belief in an arrow of time as real?" I asked. "Whether or not the discussion focuses on some form of determinism or indeterminism and the degrees of freedom to move within these poles?"

"While I might agree on the whole with that statement," said Neatono, "some philosophies and religions posit a predetermined universe, whose past and future events are strictly predetermined."

"Even so," I replied, "their basis relies on our experience that a past and future are real, do they not?" I asked.

"I would have to agree," he said.

"And can we all agree that the issue of free will is an issue that concerns only humans? The concept is meaningless for atoms or stars, as well as other biology we encounter?" I said.

"Until other biology tells us otherwise, we can all agree on that," said Sanida.

"I think that maybe you can see the outlines of where this discussion is heading," I said, "but let's continue to explore a bit further. The promise of free will lies in its power to shape one's future actions and even one's destiny, but it relies as much on our experience of the past as well, inasmuch as it allows us to overcome the limitations and challenges fate has dealt us. Ultimately though, the problem of free will is a moral one, for it is in our own and our culture's judgments regarding our actions wherein lies its importance. Are we responsible for our actions, or have they been decided for us already?"

"I can see," said Neatono, "that everything you say is correct, but, more than that, I can see that all of it is a description of reality as experienced through the lens of our own experience and relies completely on an acceptance of an arrow of time."

"Precisely," I said, "and we continually return, again and again, to the only reality we know, this biologically created experience that we believe describes reality. But what it truly describes are the things most important to us as biological beings, in one way or another. We have a deep need to reinforce our experience of reality and to quarantine it from anything that may shatter it."

"So what is the answer?" asked Sanida. "Do we abandon our senses and our minds and live in a world we have no access to?"

"I am not saying that we must abandon our experience of reality; we cannot. It is, literally, who we are and will be with us from the day we're born to the day we die. But we can now see that it is also a veil that stands between the totIs universe and us. We now have a choice. We can continually attempt to reinforce our experience of reality and deny the reality of the totIs universe, a circuitous route that will lead nowhere, or we can finally understand that our experience of reality does not allow us to experience totIs reality at all. I suggest that from this point on we stop trying to defend our viewpoints based on our experience and try to discover that which is hidden from us."

"But then aren't we just living a lie," asked Geraki, "if knowing more exists, yet we simply live with these illusions?"

"This reality we experience is the perfect one for us, for our situation, and for our relationship with the totIs universe. It is our reality and it affords us all we need to live full and satisfied lives. To abandon it would be an abandonment of ourselves, and that would lead, ultimately, to death. No, nothing changes with regard to who we are and how we live, given the tools we have with which to accomplish that," I said.

"Then of what use is this knowledge, if it changes nothing?" he asked.

"I did not say this knowledge changes nothing. I said nothing changes with regard to who we are and how we live. Do you see? We are not the center of the universe, as your hasty conclusion would pretend. I, like you, must live in this state, and I, like you, cannot see the future, nor can I see what changes this knowledge will bring about. But I do know that the totIs universe is not constrained by my situation. Its nature is not influenced by my limitations. I, for one, revel in the thought of a totIs universe, whole, complete, and perfect, one in which my place, if I can call it that, is both an integral part and connected to everything else. If there is a paradise, then this is it," I said.

TWELVE

"Socrates," said Neatono, "thank you for this gift of knowledge that offers me some freedom from the worry and misery of time's ravages and cruelty. In the totIs universe, I am still the infant who is loved and cherished by his mother, the child who is cared for and educated by his parents and mentors, the athlete reveling in the games, and the statesman helping to guide his state and his world. These are part of the totIs universe, now and always."

"That is a powerful vision, my friend," I said. "And it reflects your deeper understanding of your experience and its relationship to the totIs universe. We wonder why we experience an egg falling from the counter to the floor and breaking, but we never experience the reverse, broken eggs jumping from the floor to the counter and putting themselves back together. For us there is meaning to this reality, and that meaning is glued to our experience of time's ineluctable march forward. But, in the totIs universe where all time appeared in null time; there is no movement in it, so there is no movement at all. Nothing 'happened' first, or last. The condition we experience as the falling egg is, in the totIs universe, a texture or ripple in its body, and it cannot be altered. There is no movement through time or anywhere else; in totIs, that is a meaningless concept. The question of which came first, chicken or egg, likewise, is meaningless; they came together with the big bang and the big crunch."

"Socrates," Miapetra chimed in, "I remember you saying that in the totIs universe there are no probabilities, and I can see that in a totIs universe, where there is neither past nor future, that probability is a meaningless concept. So it would seem that probability would be a creation of our biochemistry as well. Do you think this is true of all mathematics?"

"This is an excellent question," I replied. "We are astounded by the accuracy of the ability of mathematics to describe and predict the world we experience, but we know not whence such predictive ability comes. The world of mathematics seems to be a place that exists outside of our personal experience of reality, with the added benefit that it allows us to quantify and, ultimately, manipulate matter and energy. But all the miracles of mathematics really stem from one place, and that is our perspective, the human observer's perspective."

"Are there any other perspectives or sources of information from which we can gain a view to reality outside of our experience of it?" asked Miapetra.

"There seem to be very few indeed," I replied, "but like the phenomenon of quantum entanglement, they do pierce the veil occasionally. But, if the totIs universe exists in a state of rest, not change, and space and time combine to form an ever stable and unchanging unity, then the only thing mathematics, as developed, can be describing is the experience of the world created by our biology, an experience of a dynamic and ever-changing universe."

"Why am I not surprised?" remarked Miapetra. "Yet I'm still surprised, because these two realities seem so completely different."

"Is that so?" I asked. "Is it any more surprising or different, do you think, from those who believed in a geocentric universe, or a flat earth, or that the world was created by a divine being in six days? They too were surprised by the difference between their experiences of reality and the new revealed truth of it. If that is what your experience tells you, and you can rely on it as biology, then it is real. Ultimately, these experiences of reality obtain their being in the totIs universe itself. Not a single illusion we subscribe to will change the nature of the totIs universe. It is the only complete set of everything there is and is unchanging. These earlier peoples created their own formulas and ciphering to measure and parse their known universe. We now do the same, but as long as we dissect and measure a universe of moving parts, traveling through time and space, the origins of that knowledge and its inventions will continue to be created through the biological experience that does the same. What I'm trying to get at is that the so-called realities you detail are not what's different; it's the perspectives from which we experience the totIs universe that are different."

"The discipline of mathematics is not solely concerned with describing so-called reality," said Neatono. "It is also a discipline of purely abstract thought. Is it possible that some forms of mathematics can be used to describe the totIs universe?"

"Let's not forget Bell's inequality, the EPR experiment, the double-slit experiment with and without delayed choice, all relied on higher abstract thinking and mathematics. They still describe a universe where time marches on, but reveal the underlying reality of a totIs universe. However, I don't want to debate the question of the reality of numbers or mathematics in general. I do think, however, that, if mathematics did not describe natural phenomena we experience so accurately, it would not have the power or the hold on us that it does."

Neatono said, "This reminds me of Einstein's famous quote, 'Reality is merely an illusion, albeit a very persistent one.'"

"And we can see by this discussion how true that quote is," I said, "because the illusion is a nearly perfect one, as we defined perfect illusions previously. Every time the veracity of our biologically manufactured experience is questioned, our minds turn back on themselves to try to reinforce that image of reality. At this point, perhaps it is useful to create a word that describes the biochemically created reality of the human experience used by humans as a proxy for the unknown nature of reality itself. Neatono, do you have any suggestions?"

"As our discussion has progressed, I've already begun thinking of just such a word, as it has become cumbersome to my mind to continually repeat the phrase 'biochemically produced experience of reality,'" said Neatono.

"And what have you come up with?" I asked.

"I thought of combining the Greek word for perception, that is, *antilipsi*, with *Is*, as I did with totIs, to come up with *antIs*, the *s* again sounding more like a *z* as in the word *is*," he said.

"That is good," I said. "We now have two new definitions relating to the universe and the nature of its reality. One, antIs, is defined as the human observer's experience of reality and the universe through the biochemical sensory input and interpretation system, as we've described. It also describes the near-perfect illusion this system creates and our continuous attempts to use this interpretation as a proxy for actual reality, even though it is not. Can we all agree on this definition of antIs?" I asked.

"We most certainly can agree," said Neatono.

"And," I continued, "we have the second definition, totIs, which defines a total reality of the universe unavailable to human observer's created antIs reality. TotIs describes a universe created whole and complete outside of time, as we know it. This reality and this universe appeared in null time, and so it is complete in every sense. Its beginning, middle, and end are. They, and all space, time, matter, and energy exist and are one unity. Parenthetically, antIs is a part of the totIs universe, even while totIs is unavailable to the experience provided by antIs.

THIRTEEN

As the discussion continued, brothers Nikitis and Oachyronas prepared some food and drink to help keep us grounded that we might sustain ourselves and proceed without interruption.

"Socrates," said Sanida, "it would seem that just about everything we know of the universe comes through antIs knowledge."

"This is quite true," I said, "and the weight of this knowledge acts like a proof of its own veracity, but that is not so. Like a fun-house mirror, the true shape of an object will never be revealed, no matter how many myriad snapshots from varying angles and resolutions we obtain. In this case, the lens used to amass that circumstantial evidence is unable to access the actual evidence that stands before it."

"And yet you have given us a glimpse of this totIs universe, using the antIs knowledge," said Sanida.

"As I said before, the antIs universe is built on a nearly perfect illusion, but not perfect. While our continued development of scientific knowledge has been built through the use of our antIs experience, the illusory nature of that experience is revealed in the irreconcilable results that every so often reveal themselves," I replied. "It is the ability to acknowledge those rare results for what they are, and, breaking with the tradition of trying to reconcile them with the illusions of our antIs knowledge, to seek the truth beyond those illusions."

"It is almost as if you've been able to show us the curves that form the fun-house mirror, so that we can compensate for them to see a truer image," said Sanida.

"An interesting metaphor," I replied, "for as I've pointed out before, the one constant in our antIs universe is an observer. In fact, the connection of an observer to the antIs universe is so strong that when physicists have proposed their most creative and elemental thought experiments into the nature of the universe, no matter how much is taken out of the universe for their purposes, the observer remains."

"What kind of experiments are you talking about?" asked Miapetra.

"Let's look at the essence of what the experiments are trying to do rather than the experiments themselves," I said. "Einstein, upon landing in New York City in 1919, was asked by a reporter to give a succinct explanation of relativity for the readers. Einstein replied, 'It was formerly believed that if all material things disappeared out of the universe, time and space would be left. According to the relativity theory, however, time and space disappear together with the things.' How do we know if space and time disappear? Because an observer must be left to authenticate such a result, even theoretically. Einstein considered this answer as a kind of joke, because it is, of course, impossible to accomplish this feat. Nevertheless, it shows the inherent and unconscious bias in these and nearly all other experiments."

"And as we've seen," said Neatono, "observers are in the business of interpreting reality through an antIs lens."

"Precisely," I replied, "and the upshot of it all is to anthropomorphize the universe as a whole, to make it fit in to our antIs view.

"There is another interesting phenomenon in the relativistic and quantum antIs worlds that has to do with photons—their age and the space they travel through," I continued. "Relativity shows that a photon leaving a source, say a star that is ten light years away, and traveling through the vacuum of space, will not pass through either the dimension of time or space. Until the moment it is absorbed by your eye, it will have traveled, according to its own reference frame, zero meters in zero time. However, once it is absorbed, a real distance and time can be measured by the observer."

"So can we call this a problem of framing—that is, a problem of using an antIs view of the universe?" asked Neatono.

"I believe we can," I answered. "And if we do, we can reframe the question using a totIs view."

"And what would the question be?" asked Neatono.

"Quite simply, the question would be, 'What is the totIs nature of space and time?'" I said.

"We know," said Neatono, "that in the antIs world we don't actually measure time. We measure events moving through a moment we call now. We also know that those measurements are arbitrary and mutable, depending on the reference frames of observers moving at different speeds and directions in space; there are many nows relative to one another."

"And in the totIs universe?" I asked.

"Time does not flow at all, as no time in the totIs universe existed before or after any other," he said. "All time was created in null time, and there exists no now moment in totIs."

"But what exactly might be the nature of time?" I asked.

"You have given a clue by positing that it may be a kind of solidifier, an element that stabilizes and fixes the totIs universe in place, so to speak," he replied.

"And there is a formulation in physics called a Minkowski space that theorizes the three dimensions of space with an added dimension of time, much like the space-time loaf of Brian Greene," I said. "And it is part of the basis of Einstein's and other physicists' beliefs that time, and, for that matter, reality or antIs reality, is an illusion.

"And what about space?" I asked. "What do we know about it?"

"From an antIs perspective, relativity tells us that space and time are intimately connected, as your example of the ageless photon moving through null space shows. That every point in space is the center of the universe, which is expanding in all directions, and that it is deformable by matter and energy," said Neatono.

"Indeed," I said, "and according to quantum mechanics, subatomic 'empty' space is a virtual hotbed of activity; because of the uncertainty principle, empty space is roiling with activity at the Plank length and below," I said.

"But does the antIs perspective give us an answer as to what space actually is?" I asked.

"We know we can measure it, but what we are measuring no one really knows," answered Neatono.

"AntIs space is measured in distance, which is dependent on velocity and time, and, given our antIs knowledge of these variables, we know that the antIs universe is a very big place," I said. "But what about the totIs universe? What can we say about space there?"

"Like time and everything else, it appeared in null time," said Neatono. "All of it, from its antIs emergence from the singularity to its unfathomable antIs end. As a totIs, its nature would be static, as it is combined with time, but it seems difficult to imagine its antIs properties expanding into infinity and relating that to a static totIs universe," he said.

"Even though we have these new definitions of totIs and antIs to help us, our vocabulary is still extremely limited and primitive when it relates to totIs concepts, and so we will continue to conflate the two perspectives, even as we try to tease them apart," I said.

"But before we ask, 'What is totIs space?'" I continued, "we should ask, 'How big is totIs space?'"

"It would seem to be quite large indeed," said Neatono, "especially totIs space, as it incorporates all space throughout all time. It could very well be infinite."

"And yet a speeding photon can collapse this infinite space to a null property," I replied. "What separates points in space? Are there discrete points separate from one another? How do we know how distant such points are from one another, given space's ability to collapse in the reference frame of a photon? Like time, space too is known to us only through our antIs experience. Since we've seen that this antIs experience of time is illusory, what makes us think that our antIs experience of space is any different?" I asked.

"Of course it would not be, would it?" Sanida said rhetorically.

"In the totIs universe, the idea of measuring time is meaningless, since all points in time appeared together. There is no before or after to be found.

With an inability to measure time, how do we measure space, which, likewise, appeared together?" I asked. "So the answer to how big space is appears to be that we cannot know."

"Are you saying that the space we inhabit might be very tiny or even larger than we see?" asked Neatono.

"I am saying that measuring space, like measuring time, is meaningless in the totIs universe," I said. "How big, how far, how much time are all antIs experiences that only have meaning to our biology. The totIs universe is time-less and spaceless, in the sense that measuring it has no meaning, nor does it offer a description of it."

"Then it is hopeless to gain a firsthand experience of this totIs universe," said Sanida.

"Well, let's try," I said. "Let's close our eyes and relax as best we can. Try to imagine that you—that is, the observer who you are—do not exist. There is no longer a biofeedback loop and so no sensory experience at all. From this null state, can you discover anything?" I asked.

After a moment, Neatono cried, "This is impossible! I just can't make myself disappear! I can't believe that just because I don't exist that the universe doesn't exist."

"I'm not saying that the universe doesn't exist if you don't. It's your experi-ence of the universe that doesn't exist without you, and without that, you have no access to the universe at all," I said.

"To get back to your other point," said Sanida, "if space and time are un-measurable, and the entirety of the totIs universe appeared in null time, then every atom, every quark that comprises this universe, are in their place, fixed forever."

"Yes," I said, "except the forever part, that can't be measured, as you so rightly pointed out."

"Every thought, every action, every nuance of emotion and meaning is fixed in space and time, unchanging," he continued. "How absolutely impos-sible that is for me to believe."

"Would it be easier to believe if there were no biology, only inanimate atoms, photons, and all other matter and energy that was fixed in this totIs universe?" I asked. "They have no need for time, space, nor anything else to comport with some experience of reality that they call theirs."

"If the universe were made of only inanimate material, I guess it wouldn't matter at all. We wouldn't even be having this discussion," Sanida replied.

"At the same time, every part of the totIs universe is integral to and inseparable from its totIs. All exist in the same frame of unity. As biology, from our antIs perspectives, we are immortal! Surely there's some solace in that?" I asked.

"I guess there's some," said Neatono, "but it's purely theoretical to me, as my experience is ineluctably leading me to my demise."

"To use the metaphor of music, that's true if you're talking about notes being played, but the score is immortal," I replied. "Does a symphonic piece cease to exist when the symphony has finished playing and gone home?" I asked.

"I see your point," said Neatono. "You have a perspective that refuses to be cornered or boxed in, and I'm glad of it. Thank you."

"The ramifications of a totIs universe are momentous, and if we can integrate them with our own antIs experience, the limitations of our biology and our perspective become less burdensome and limiting," I replied.

"But, Socrates," Sanida broke in, "aren't you talking about the block universe theory here, and the ideas of the eternalists?" he asked.

"I will admit that what is being described here has a common theme to the idea of a block universe," I replied, "but I have not set out to prove or disprove any particular theory. What I have attempted to do is to set aside, once and for all, the observer's viewpoint—that is, the antIs experience of the universe—so that whatever the reality of this universe actually is might have the ability to emerge. As we can see, that is a nearly impossible thing to do."

"But couldn't you have started with a block universe theory and worked back to our subjective imprint on the universe, as we know it?" he asked.

"If I was trying to prove the block universe theory, I might have done that," I said, "but the fact is, what I needed to expose is not only the illusory nature of the antIs experience, but the inferior quality of its representation as well. What I mean by inferior is that it is of a level both removed and inaccessible to the actual nature of the totIs universe. Like a moth to a flame, we would, and will, continually revolve around and around our profound faith in the ultimate integrity of the antIs experience and rely on it as axiomatic to all our explorations."

"But, certainly, much has already been explored regarding the nature of reality in a block universe," said Sanida. "Is there something there that we can partake of?"

"To my mind, even the brilliant formulations of the block universe proponents like JJC Smart, Hermann Minkowski, Hilary Putnam, and Roger Penrose, lay their foundations on the bedrock of the antIs experience of reality. In fact, the need for the creation of the block universe, whose scientific roots spring from relativity, by the way, comes itself from its meaning for determinism and predeterminism—that is, free will. Causality, too, is an important feature in explaining the block universe, but we've seen that the totIs universe has no past or future events; there is no causality when all appears in null time. Causality is our antIs illusion, and as such is unshakable to us in its position for interpreting that reality, but what we have begun to describe is a totIs universe that is atemporal, acausal, of indeterminate size, static, stable, and a unity."

"This whole discussion began with the question of whether our experience of time reflects the true nature of time," said Neatono, "and we can see the effects of that question here."

"Truly," I replied, "for the time we experience, or what we can call antIs time, is quite unlike totIs time. Its movement, along with the rest of the revealed universe, which that movement creates, is an illusion. In totIs time, there is no movement, and it seems that using the word *time* to describe it only causes more confusion."

"You are right; we are like moths to a flame," said Neatono. "My experience of our discussion is that it seems to be created as we go, free flowing and unknowable. Yet, if this is an illusion and totIs is the actual universe, it's all here all the time. These are truly irreconcilable facts."

"As far as we know," said Sanida, "humans are the only observers, in the sense we're talking about, that we know of in the entire universe. Look at what we've accomplished with that ability to be an observer—science, art, architecture, politics, and economics—it goes on and on. All this has been accomplished using the natural and abstract laws we've discovered, and those laws are based on time's movement and causality," he said.

"And to me that is part of the wonder of the totIs universe; all this, and so much more, is part and parcel of its body, for lack of a better term. All these accomplishments, as well as all the accomplishments of the inanimate universe itself, are the textures and shadings of this unified totIs reality," I said. "If you remember our definition of a perfect illusion, that is what our antIs experience is, except for us today where it has become imperfect, if only just barely. This is the reason it is so difficult to reconcile the two; the urge to maintain this illusion as a perfect one is as primal as all our other biological urges."

FOURTEEN

"Neatono, what say you now about your animus toward time?" I asked. "As you promised," he replied, "I have learned much. And also, as promised, it is not what I expected."

"And have you found some solace or peace with your feelings?" I asked.

"In a purely theoretical way, I have come to appreciate that my feelings are a function of my inability to experience totIs reality, but as a conscious being I am still left with the same fears and distaste for my antis experience of times ravages," he replied.

"Are you surprised by this fact?" I asked.

"I guess I am looking for a balm that will effectively pacify my anxieties," he said.

"So understanding that our experience of time's arrow is an interpretation of totIs time, which appears as a function of our biochemistry and the processing of its interaction with totIs time to create a now moment through which time appears to flow, is not useful in helping you allay your fears?" I asked.

"As a conscious individual, it does not mollify me," he replied.

"Consciousness, what is that?" I asked.

"It is my awareness of myself and the world around me," he replied.

"And would you agree that we could call you or any conscious being who is aware of himself or herself and their surroundings to be an observer—which is a term we've been using quite a bit in our discussion?" I asked.

"As a general definition, that would be accurate," said Neatono.

"And from whence does this observer appear?" I asked.

"Well that's the sixty-four-thousand-dollar question, isn't it!" he exclaimed.

"Indeed it is," I replied, "and it has been a question for as long as mankind has had consciousness."

"There are, of course, many theories and beliefs on the subject," he said, "which usually tend toward the mystic or religious when it isn't looked at as a purely biochemical process."

"Very true," I replied. "And when it is looked at as a purely physical manifestation—that is, as a product of matter, biology, and biochemistry—the answers are most unsatisfying, because they show no artifact by which consciousness appears out of the machinery," I said.

"This is true," said Neatono. "And is why, I think, the divine interpretations of consciousness hold the greatest sway with humanity."

"Indeed," I said. "Though atheists and scientists seek an answer outside the realm of divine creation and blind faith."

"But, for us normal people, these ideas are unsatisfactory, and the divine or mystic interpretations are more satisfying," said Neatono.

"And the divine interpretations have the added force of placing consciousness above, or more precisely, at the center of, mere pedestrian reality," I said. "And this is what reinforces the antIs perfect illusion in our experience of reality."

"So are you saying that consciousness is an illusion?" asked Neatono.

"We have been using the word *illusion* to describe the antIs experience, because we showed its connection to the myriad phenomenon we describe as illusions in our everyday life," I said. "But to call the antIs experience an illusion is inaccurate, as it itself is part of totIs, and as such cannot be an illusion per se. Indeed, illusions, as we've been using the term, can be considered functions dependent on the biosensory systems and their relationship to the reality at their base."

"And are you saying that consciousness is just such a function as well?" asked Neatono.

"Before I answer that," I replied, "I will ask whether you agree that the entirety of the antIs experience flows from the single fact that we experience time as flowing through a now moment?"

"That is kind of hard to answer," replied Neatono. "I'm racking my brain here, but it does seem that all our experiences depend on time's movement."

"If you remember our failed attempt to imagine that we don't exist, and to see if we could experience the universe outside of an antIs experience, I think we have our answer," I said.

"We will agree, then," said Neatono, "that the flow of time through a created now moment is at the base of all antIs experience."

"Then the only thing left to describe is the observer of the antIs experience," I said.

"But whence does he or she come?" cried Neatono.

"The observer, too, like the seeming flow of time, appears with the creation of the now moment on which antIs reality is built," I said.

"Can you make that clearer?" asked Neatono.

"I'll try," I replied. "Biology's interpretation of time's flow through a now moment brings into being an entire antIs universe specific to, and within, the biology of the organism that creates it. This now moment is a function of the relationship of the biochemistry producing the antIs experience to totIs reality."

"I can see that." Said Neatono.

"Consciousness, then, is a function of the antIs now moment in relation to the antIs reality it engenders."

"So you are saying that consciousness has its foundation in the antIs now moment?" he asked.

"I'm saying that consciousness is a function of another function we call the now moment, whose basis is ultimately totIs. Consciousness, being a function of the now moment, ceases to be when that now moment ceases to be. This is the reason we can find and study the machinery and processes of life and cognition but not consciousness itself. Why? Because we can never discover the source of consciousness, as it is a function of the very now moment we are using to search for it. Consciousness exists in the 'space'—if you will—created by the now moment and the antIs universe it appears in, and is inseparable from it. As the saying goes, no matter how sharp the knife, it can never cut itself."

"Then consciousness is but an illusion!" exclaimed Neatono.

"There are no illusions in the totIs universe," I said. "What we call illusions are simply unexpected outcomes from seemingly straightforward events. But, if we, perchance, inspect the source of the illusion, we see that it is based on our limited perspective and the operating limits of our senses. What we experience and who we are, though from an antIs source, are integral parts of the totIs universe. But make no mistake; we are not the center of that universe. Indeed, we occupy a place of limited access to its totality."

"And so consciousness, unable to exist except in the presence—which sounds strangely like a field—of a now moment, will have to experience absolutely everything through that presence, or cease to be. Brilliant!" said Sanida. "Now we see why the observer is the center of the antIs universe and its myriad phenomena."

FIFTEEN

"So where do we go from here?" asked Neatono.

"Perhaps we should all go home," I said. "It's been a challenging but fruitful afternoon, and I think we are getting tired."

"But I'm still interested in this wave-particle duality that lies at the heart of QM," he said. "Can we integrate this duality in the totIs universe?" he asked.

"I think there's a way to look at it from outside of the antIs results and put it in a totIs universe," I said, "but what do you think?"

"With a static and stable totIs universe, there would be no waves, as a wave propagates through antIs time," he said.

"Let's not forget that, to describe the totIs universe as static and/or stable, still uses antIs conceptions. TotIs is a unity with a capital *U*," I replied. "The terms *static* and *stable* both denote states relative to time."

"But we have no words that denote reality without a reference to time," said Sanida.

"We do have totIs," I said, "but let's just be cognizant of the fact that, when we speak of the state of the totIs universe, time does not function as we experience it in our antIs way."

"We can only try," said Neatono.

"So, as we've seen," I continued, "to speak about the age of the totIs universe is meaningless, as what we call time within it doesn't flow at all. Additionally, to speak about its size is likewise meaningless, as there is nothing within or without of totIs by which we can make a meaningful measurement. But we also know that our antIs experiences are functions, ultimately, of a totIs reality, so we've been looking in the antIs experience for the items and phenomena that make up the totIs universe."

"Socrates," said Sanida, "this sounds very much like the situation represented in the allegory of the cave that was so well illustrated by your student Plato. The shadows we see are an antIs reflection on the wall of the cave, which is our reality, but the light that casts that reflection is the totIs universe itself."

"I think my good pupil Plato would endorse your finding," I replied.

"But let's get back to the QM conundrum," said Neatono. "To account for the wave-particle duality, we'd need to find a conception that does not have a flow of time because, in essence, waves do not exist in totIs."

"True," I said, "and to do this, we would need a conceptualization, as described earlier, of the totIs universe as existing in some kind of solid form and exhibiting something like a texture. We can further conceptualize it, as previously alluded to, as a kind of Minkowski space, except that the world lines and light cones that are central to Minkowski spaces do not depict time's movement, but its mass, so to speak."

"The world line and its accompanying light cone in Minkowski space would be a representation from the antIs point of view then?" asked Neatono.

"The totIs universe has no need for light cones," I replied, "as they are functions of time's movement. Instead, the entire totIs universe becomes a kind of Minkowski solid, a complete unity, and the antIs events we experience become, in totIs, textures within that solid. I think we can combine the antIs wave-particle duality into a single reality by asking, 'How fine is the texture of totIs unity?'"

"How do we find a texture in a timeless and spaceless universe?" asked Neatono.

"I admit that this is difficult." I replied. "But the fact is, the universe we experience is not the totIs universe. These conceptualizations are not the reality of totIs but an analogy that gives us a way to see something closer to its essence," I replied.

"Yes," said Sanida. "I can conceptualize a totIs universe where time acts to hold together all of space as well as matter and energy, which, in this totIs universe, will not be dynamic but will instead act as a kind of texture, as you've described."

"And even though the questions of how long or how far are meaningless in this totIs universe, the question of the resolution, for lack of a better word, of this totIs universe is possible," I said. "I think we can look at wavelength in the antIs universe as the resolution or graininess in the body of the totIs universe. Looking through our biologically created filter of a now through which time moves, the finer the grain in the totIs universe, the higher the frequency of the antIs wavelength."

"In this conception, as Sanida just said," said Neatono, "it seems that time unifies and congeals all space, matter, and energy—indeed, all the contents of this universe, whether known or unknown to us."

"That would be an excellent way to describe it," I replied.

"And another casualty of the antIs universe would be our experience of cause and effect," he stated.

"Most assuredly," I replied, "for our experience of cause and effect in the antIs universe is part and parcel of our experience of a flow of time through a now moment. This experience is part of the illusion by which reality is made manifest to us. It is the only doorway we have, as observers, through which we are able to experience reality."

"I find it quite interesting," said Sanida, "that there is, within the human psyche, a prescient acknowledgment of fate as an actuality, an uneasy feeling that all is written. Free will becomes the antidote to such feelings, but as with all religious and mystical thought, we must simply have faith in its truth, for there is no proof of its existence."

"From the antIs perspective," I replied, "fate, fatalism, and the block universe of the eternalists is a deplorable situation, but we must remember that fate requires time to flow, which, in the totIs universe, it does not. There is neither yesterday, now, nor tomorrow, and as such there is no fate to come. We are each beyond timeless or eternal. We are integral to the very structure of the totIs universe and connected to every part of it. The great irony and conundrum is that the part of us that can realize this, our consciousness, can never experience or access it."

"And thus Einstein's famous quote," said Sanida. "'Reality is merely an illusion, albeit a very persistent one.'"

"Indeed," I said. "He could practically touch the reality of the illusion, but, alas, like us all, he was ever unable to appreciate that the illusion does not exist 'out there' but is created from within our biology itself."

FINALE

"Well, well," said Neatono, "this has been a most interesting and enlightening conversation, which could go on for a fortnight, I'm sure. But I think that you are correct, and it is time to call it a day, for though my mind is enlivened, my body wearies."

"I and my brother must leave as well, for I'm sure our cold dinner sits waiting for us at home," said Nikitis.

"And Mother will not be pleased," agreed Oachyronas, "though it was worth it to have been a part of this most amazing discussion."

"So it seems our little symposium has come to an end," I said.

"For now," said Sanida, "for there is much to think on and mull over, as I'm sure the ramifications of these ideas will become clearer and require further discussion."

"I am sure you are right," said Miapetra, "but this has been a most agreeable afternoon indeed, and I'm so glad you were able to stop by and visit with Father."

"As am I," Neatono and I replied in unison.

"And I will make sure to stop by more often so as to continue our discussions," I continued, laughing.

"Please do, dear Socrates," said Neatono, chortling, "for though my experiences of our time together may be illusory, they are nonetheless enjoyable, and I look forward to them immensely."

"And don't forget to invite the rest of us," said Sanida.

"I surely will," I replied, "for to have such open-minded, intelligent, and well-educated friends as you makes for very fruitful and enjoyable discussions."

And so our little party ended, and all departed, embarking upon the path that lay before them, reevaluating with new perspective the words of Albert Einstein as they reverberated in their minds: "Reality is merely an illusion, albeit a very persistent one."

The End

BIBLIOGRAPHY

Aczel, Amir D. *Entanglement*. New York: Four Walls Eight Windows, 2002.

Barrow, John D. *The Book of Nothing*. New York: Vintage Books, 2002.

Einstein, Albert. *Relativity, the Special and General Theory*. New York: Crown Publishers Inc., 1961.

Greene, Brian. *The Fabric of the Cosmos*. New York: Alfred A. Knopf, 2004.

Gribbin, John. *In Search of Schrödingers Cat; Quantum Physics and Reality*. New York: Bantam Books, 1984.

Gribbin, John. *Schrödingers Kittens and the Search for Reality*. New York: Little Brown and Co., 1995.

Hawking, Stephen. *A Brief History of Time*. New York: Bantam Books, 1988.

Herbert, Nick. *Quantum Reality*. New York: Anchor Books, 1985.

Krauss, Lawrence M. *A Universe from Nothing*. New York: Atria Books, 2012.

Wilber, Ken. *Quantum Questions*, Boulder, CO: Shambhala Publications Inc., 1984.

51570083R00060

Made in the USA
Charleston, SC
26 January 2016